JOHN SAEKI spends his working days writing and designing maps, charts and information graphics on world news. When he is not composing explainers on pandemics, political turmoil and endangered wildlife, he heads through woodland valleys and over the hills, looking in wonder at this strange planet we live on.

His first book, *The Tiger Hunters of Tai O*, was published by Blacksmith Books in 2017, featuring a fictional tiger in the hills of Lantau Island. After that, he went on the trail of real tigers that came to Hong Kong and found an unexpected treasure trove of forgotten history.

He now lives in windswept Yorkshire, and often talks with family and friends of the wonderful animals he came across in his 20 years in the subtropics of Hong Kong.

The Last Tigers of Hong Kong

True stories of big cats that stalked
Britain's Chinese colony

John Saeki

BLACKSMITH BOOKS

The Last Tigers of Hong Kong

ISBN 978-988-75546-1-5

Published by Blacksmith Books
Unit 26, 19/F, Block B, Wah Lok Industrial Centre,
37-41 Shan Mei Street, Fo Tan, Hong Kong
Tel: (+852) 2877 7899
www.blacksmithbooks.com

Edited by Paul Christensen
Illustrations by Gary Yeung

The author asserts the moral right to be identified as the author
of this work.

CONTENTS

China

Deep Bay

Yuen Long

△
Tai Mo Shan

△
Castle Peak

New Territories

Tsuen Wan

Tsing Yi

Mui Wo

Lantau Island

Tai O

Cheung Chau

South China Sea

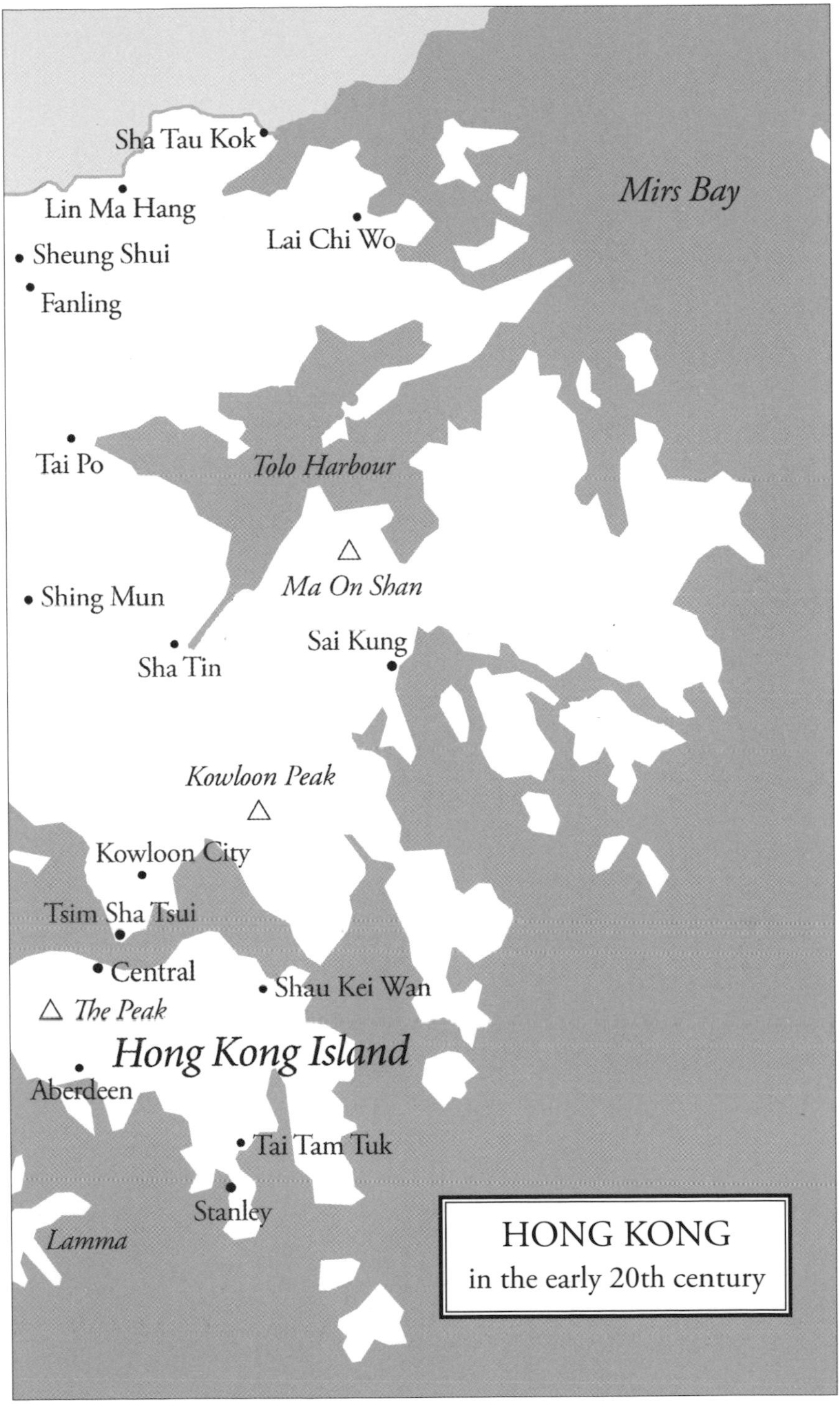

Sha Tau Kok

Mirs Bay

Lin Ma Hang

Lai Chi Wo

Sheung Shui

Fanling

Tai Po

Tolo Harbour

Shing Mun

△
Ma On Shan

Sai Kung

Sha Tin

Kowloon Peak
△

Kowloon City

Tsim Sha Tsui

Central

Shau Kei Wan

△ The Peak

Hong Kong Island

Aberdeen

Tai Tam Tuk

Stanley

Lamma

HONG KONG
in the early 20th century

THE HONG KONG TIGER LIST

As reported in the *China Mail, Hong Kong Telegraph, South China Morning Post, Hong Kong Daily Press, Hong Kong Sunday Telegraph, Hong Kong Sunday Herald* and *Hong Kong Naturalist* magazine

Tiger Bones
February 1901
A correspondent on a hunting trip in the New Territories sees the remains of a tiger.

Two Tigers Crawling
September 1902
Farmer finds three cows dead. Sits up in a tree all night to keep watch. Sees two tigers crawling, shoots, misses.

Castle Peak Tiger
1907 – 1908
Roaming feline picking off the occasional pig, carries off a cow.

The Kowloon Kangaroo
1910
Said to have eaten children, dismissed in the *China Mail*.

Kowloon Baby Eater
1910
Another one said to eat children, dismissed in the *Hong Kong Telegraph*.

Aberdeen Prowler
1910
First sighting on Hong Kong Island, this time from "unimpeachable sources" they say.

1911 Stanley Tiger
March – August
Roamed all around slaughtering livestock including on Hong Kong Island, Lamma and Lantau.

Leaping Tiger
1912
Jumps onto the road near Deep Water Bay golf course.

Pig Thief of Sai Kung
1912
Makes off with a porker.

Tai Tam Tuk Target
1912
Indian policeman has tiger in his sights, misses.

1914 Peak Tiger
March – May
Many stories, witnesses including from the European top brass. Fifty-soldier hunting party in April. Rumours of a "coolie" killed.

Sheung Shui Tiger
First appeared January 1915. **KILLED** on 8th March
PC Ernest Goucher followed up local reports, found the tiger, was attacked, and died in hospital four days later. PC Rutton Singh was also killed in the follow up hunting party. Tiger eventually shot by Donald Burlingham. Displayed at City Hall.

1916 Castle Peak Tiger
Carried off a pig. Local fired two shots. Missed.

1916 Sha Tau Kok Tiger
Grass cutter saw a tiger eating a cow. Hunting party found a mutilated carcass.

1916 Peak Tiger
Spotted at Magazine Nullah and Bowen Road. Peak tram passengers heard a roar. Seen from houses and gardens on the Peak. Indignant letters to the press.

Fanling Golf Club Tigers
1918
Seen by golfers and the caretaker who tracked the "beasts", plural, to bushes and "commanded" Chinese workers to wade in. Workers refused. Tiger disappeared.

The Pat Heung Valley Tiger
1918
Cows missing in several villages, carcasses found. One witness reported two large adults and three cubs.

The Temple Tiger of Kowloon
1919
Appeared to worshippers in the temple and then disappeared.

1925 Sha Tau Kok Tiger
Back and forth over the border, killing livestock. Locals requested help from the HK police.

Repulse Bay Hotel Tiger
1925
Two ladies staying at the hotel saw a tiger prowling up and down the

beach. Or perhaps they didn't, according to the men.

Kowloon Peak Tiger
December 1925
Witnessed on Kowloon side by six European ramblers on a day trip.

Lee Garden Tiger
1926
Live tiger caught in a snare in Shatin. Displayed at Lee Hysan's Lee Garden Amusement Park.

Wanchai Gap Tiger
1927
Seen by the "house boy" of No. 264 The Peak at Wanchai Gap as he was returning from market.

1927 Kowloon Tiger
Seen by Europeans and Chinese. Farmers lost pigs and poultry.

Ship's Mascot
1928
Six-week-old cub for sale at a market on Hong Kong Island. Looked after by the superintendent of the Botanical and Forestry Department. Later it boarded *HMS Cumberland* – as ship's mascot.

1929 New Territories Tiger
Cow killed. A hunter ties up a goat and waits with his gun.

Tai Po Tiger Family
1930
Tigress with two cubs seen near Tai Po Market.

Tsing Yi Tiger
1930
Tiger on the island, seen to kill and make off with a pig.

Brickworks Tiger
1931
Driver on the Castle Peak Road spots tiger. Farmer's pig killed.

Chun Cheng Tiger
1932
Leaves three cow carcasses on a hillside with deep claw marks and throats torn out.

Ting Kau District Tiger
1932
Spotted by two Indian police officers.

Tao Fung Shan Tiger
1933
Crossing the valley below the monastery.

Pereira's Tiger
1934
Witnessed by R.A. Pereira and two companions on a bird hunt in hills near Tsuen Wan.

1934 Kowloon Tiger
Walks through the centre of a village.

The Ma On Shan Marauder
1935 – 1936
Series of reports spanning months. Sometimes the "Marauder" was more than one animal. Hunts organised. Rumours of a human mauling.

Sai Kung Buffalo Slaughterer
September 1936
Five dead buffaloes in Sai Kung, slashed with tiger claws.

The Tai Wai Rambler
1937
Woman killed, reduced to blood-stained remains on the north east face of Tai Mo Shan, with "nearly the whole of her body missing". Wood collector headed up hill, never seen again.

Sham Shui Po Dog Chaser
1938
Seen crossing a vegetable plantation, chasing a dog, at 2:30 in the afternoon.

Tiger on the Eve of War
1941
Spotted at the Peak and at Tai Tam.

The Stanley Tiger
1942
Outside Stanley prison camp. Officially the last tiger **KILLED** in Hong Kong. Skin hangs at Stanley Tin Hau Temple.

1946 Tai Mo Shan Tiger
Footprints on the mountain side.

Lai Chi Wo Tiger
1947
Killed a cow, pig and dog

1947 Tao Fung Shan Tiger
Slaughtered a water buffalo

Lin Ma Hang Tiger
1948
Policeman took a shot.

Border Tiger Duo
1948
Two seen crossing back into the mainland.

Railway Tunnel Tiger
1948
Leaves pig carcass at the mouth of railway tunnel.

Tiger Trio of Ta Kwu Ling
1948
Three tigers roaming the hills near the mainland border. Bones and intestines of a pig left strewn.

Tai Wai Chuen Tiger
1948
Takes a screaming pig.

Tsuen Wan Tiger
1949
Flashlight at midnight catches sight of a striped marauder creeping into the dark.

The Lost Trophy Tiger
1949
Shot in the New Territories. Strapped to a car.

Fanling Tiger
1949
Spotted at the golf course.

Shatin Paddy Tiger
1949
Foot prints in a paddy field. Pregnant cow has stomach torn open.

Sai Kung Cow-Stalker
1949
Big cat spying on livestock.

Man-Mauler of Shatin
1949
Boar hunter finds tiger cub, ends up in hospital with broken teeth, arm and slashed legs and side.

1950 Lin Ma Hang Tiger
Killed two cows and a calf.

Nam Chung Tiger
1951
Attack on a pig near the border at Sha Tau Kok.

1952 Sai Kung Tiger
Fatal attack on buffalo triggers hunting expedition.

Cemetery Hill Tiger
1955
82-year-old grandma raises the alarm. Army Lieutenant identifies footprints.

Beast of Fierce Ghost Bridge
1959
23-year-old woman sees a sleeping tiger. A man complains of whining dogs, finds footprints. Search party sets out.

The Shing Mun Rambler
July – September 1965
A series of detailed reports including sightings, footprints, and roars. Police took it seriously, as did the HKU biology department. Triggers several hunts over weeks. Possibly the last tiger of Hong Kong.

INTRODUCTION

THE TIGERS OF HONG KONG

Tigers came to Hong Kong.

They appeared frequently and scared people, though their sightings were always fleeting. They would flash through the undergrowth, stride across hillsides and trample over farmland.

They left signs – huge paw prints and mighty roars in the night. They preyed on pigs, chickens, cattle and deer. They left calling-cards of torn flesh.

They also killed people.

When they visited, they were at the top of the food chain, except for one species, a species that appears to have been spectacularly successful, a species that won the war against tigers, yet always seems on the brink of self-destruction.

That species is us of course, humans. We invented God and said that he made us in his own image, though we cowered in fear of the stalking tiger for centuries. Eventually we made weapons that let us get the better of the big cat. Then we set out with a vengeance, and finished the tiger off in much of its territory.

To be fair, the war against tigers wasn't played out in Hong Kong. That's because Hong Kong lies on the extremity of a vast landscape. It is on the periphery of China. For a long time the area had been mostly uninteresting either to large groups of humans or to the South China tiger whose heartland lay hundreds of miles to the north in the mountainous wilderness of inland Fujian. But they both came, human migrants and vagrant tigers. Human politics put the region in the spotlight for power players, and tigers just kind of wandered in every now and then looking for free food.

Not everyone took the tiger reports seriously. The English-language press loved a tiger story, but just to ensure no one would take them to be fools, they also loved to scorn a tiger claim. There was a racist tendency to treat a local Chinese claim with more scepticism than a claim made by an Englishman. And a sexist tendency to take a man's word to be of more value than a woman's. If a Westerner of good standing couldn't corroborate a claim there was a chance that the witness was too excitable, or had mistaken a civet cat, monkey, pig or dog for the Lord of the Hundred Beasts. On the other hand, if a European, or better still a British person, a man especially, with a good job, like a clerk, a civil servant or, best of all, a policeman or high-ranking army officer, reported one – well then, it goes down as fact.

The intriguing thing is that despite the existence of testimony from people who qualified according to the above criteria, Hong Kong tigers still didn't make it into the history books, other than the two most famous tigers killed here. Of course history is about what people do to each other and there is so much to say about that, so perhaps it is understandable that natural history is usually edited out. But history is also about how we live and the conditions we live in. If a tiger is in your neighbourhood, that has an impact on your life. It affects your behaviour. You keep your kids and your old parents indoors, and your door locked. You might not be able to tend to your crops. You keep weapons at hand, you learn to be vigilant, you learn to read the signs. You don't wander about alone at night. A tiger has an impact on society, so it has an impact on history.

So why didn't tigers really make it into the mainstream narrative about Hong Kong? And by the way, if the tiger history of Hong Kong has not yet been told, what other histories are we missing?

I have a couple of ideas about the missing tiger stories.

First of all, tigers are almost invisible. Even if tiger visits were frequent in the first part of the 20th century, they tended to be fleeting. The Lord of the Hundred Beasts, to use a title American researcher Chris Coggins translated from Chinese, melts into the landscape just as quickly as it appears. There could be five sightings in a district one month, then none for a year. Tigers crouch, they almost slither on the ground. One hunter described a tiger to be like a snake. They hide and watch, they can be still for hours, though they can fly through the air. They are silent, except when they explode in a roar. They can appear from nowhere, and they can just as quickly disappear.

Another reason is prejudice. The British overlords of the colony did not expect to find magnificent big cats in the territory. They did not think they belonged here, and most of them never saw one. The British in the early part of the century didn't go out and about at night, when tigers are most active. They went to bed early and stayed behind closed doors. Only the wild and the untamed were active and restless at night, and who's going to believe their words? There was a sense that the grandeur of the tiger didn't belong to this scratty place that was not much more than a trading post and garrison town in many people's minds – hardly the jewel in the crown that was India.

Tigers are magnificent animals that belonged to the mysterious wonderland of the Indian rainforest. There, brave, mostly aristocratic hunters of renown would shoot the beasts from the backs of elephants after they were flushed out of the forest by an army of Indian jungle beaters. Tigers come at that level of power and drama, not skulking around the deforested wastelands of Hong Kong's back country, tearing off the odd limb from a buffalo or a pig.

The habits and habitat of the South China tiger were little understood especially by the outsiders from Britain and the other countries of the western world. The majority of western travellers came to China seeking profit through trade; they stuck mostly to the coast and spent little time thinking about the wildlife inland. The South China tiger was unnoticed by the average visitor to Hong Kong, Canton or Amoy. High-ranking officers and consuls, even in the trading posts of the heartlands, were just as ignorant. But the locals had a completely different story.

District offices of southern China kept detailed records of tiger encounters going back two thousand years. Coggins looked through records in the natural range of the South China tiger and realised that the beast had been everywhere inland throughout four provinces, including Guangdong, which is where Hong Kong was situated until the British prised it off.

He also counted the dead, those killed by tigers, and found documentary evidence of an estimated minimum of 10,000 people killed in 1,900 years of record keeping. His analysis shows a clear spike in casualties from the 1500s to the 1600s when human encroachment into tiger territory intensified. But this is research done in recent decades and Hong Kong's colonial political leaders and administrators of the early 20th century were oblivious to such trends.

Villagers throughout the region knew all about the Lord of the Hundred Beasts. They guarded their livestock with gongs, poles and firecrackers. They told their children to behave, and doused them in rags soaked in the blood of the beast to ward off evil and disease. They passed on wisdom such as always to run downhill when a tiger comes stalking. They locked their doors at night, and didn't write down too much history, though sometimes they ate tiger flesh.

There were some officials in Hong Kong who understood the situation better than others. Not surprisingly they were the specialists in zoology, agriculture and hunting. They knew the tigers were here, or at least that they came here on their travels. Hong Kong University biologist Geoffrey Herklots told an audience in the mid-1930s that tigers on average visited the colony once a year. He wrote much about the territory's wildlife from the late 1920s to the Japanese occupation, and the renowned biologist had no problem accepting the fact that tigers visited. As with pangolins, a favourite tiger food, it is much easier for the expert to detect the presence of the tiger than it is to actually catch a glimpse of the elusive animal. Spoors or pugs, their footprints, and the occasional roar were the main giveaways. That and the carnage they left behind when they ripped apart their prey.

The police too were familiar with the tiger's calling card, the mutilated livestock that they would occasionally be called to examine. They saw the footprints, the claw marks and some of them even caught sight of stripes and took a shot. The journalists got wind several times a year. There was no doubt an appetite for a good tiger yarn, but so often the hacks reported the details they had been told with a nod and a wink, details that were consistent throughout the decades, year after year. But of course they would only know that if they checked the archives.

The westerner who got to know the South China tiger better than any other outsider was an American missionary. Harry Caldwell arrived in the region a seasoned hunter, but he had never seen a tiger until he set foot in China. When the villagers he came to serve in the Fujianese hinterland saw how Caldwell worked his gun on the local fauna, they told him about the man-eating tigers and begged him to set his sights on them. Caldwell soon discovered that killing a tiger was more effective at converting people to Jesus than any sermon on the mount. By the time he left China in the chaos of Japanese invasion he had killed 48 of the beasts. His exploits in what seemed like far-off exotic lands were occasionally mentioned in Hong Kong press reports, though perhaps the readers were blissfully unaware of the fact that members of the same species as those man-eaters Caldwell dispatched were frequent visitors in their neighbourhoods.

In Hong Kong, history buffs agree on at least two undisputed tiger apparitions that happened in 1915 and 1942. We know about the first tiger because the beast killed two policemen, one an Englishman called Ernest Goucher from Nottinghamshire, and the other Rutton Singh from India. The tiger was also killed and its body was displayed at City Hall for all to see. Its head now survives in the police museum at Wanchai Gap, if the records are correct. Just weeks before the 1915 tragedy, reports of a tiger in the vicinity were treated with the usual mix of sensation and scepticism. Once there were bodies, the doubters shut up, for a short time, until scepticism crept back in again.

The other tiger killed in the territory met its fate nearly 30 years later. You can see its skin for yourself, hanging over an altar in the Tin Hau temple at Stanley, ragged and tattered, mostly a dirty dark brown, like a bearskin, but you can make out the stripes if you look closely. Its story is shrouded in the fog of war as it was shot in 1942 when Hong Kong was under Japanese occupation, and record-keeping was in tatters. But there are accounts of it from former prisoners at Stanley who recalled the shooting party that went after the beast.

This tiger remains controversial as several accounts suggest that the big cat killed wasn't wild, but was a circus escapee. Judging by the frequent reports up to the wartime period, and in the decade following the Japanese surrender, there is no reason to think that the escapee theory is any more convincing than that of a wild tiger. Herklots, who was at the Stanley camp at the time, certainly had no difficulty in accepting the fact that it was a genuine wild tiger.

To many with a passing interest in the subject, those two incidents are the extent of tiger lore in Hong Kong. Yet not only have I seen scores of accounts in the period between those two incidents, the reports continued to appear in the press until well into the 1950s. In fact the latest credible account comes from 1965. Considering that tiger experts estimate there were still around 1,000 South China tigers in the wild in the 1960s, I find the 1965 report plausible, even if it isn't proven. So did the police and Gurkha units at the time that spent several nights up in trees around Shing Mun Reservoir and beyond, trying, unsuccessfully, to catch the elusive beast.

After that time, if any tiger reached Hong Kong, they would have been escapees from Mao's war against the species, which the Communist Party declared a pest and a hindrance to the country's development goals. Party loyalists formed themselves into tiger brigades and went out slaughtering as many of the creatures as they could, using machine guns and grenades as well as traditional hunting rifles and crossbows. They were encouraged by government buyout schemes for skins, which guaranteed prices and supplied an export trade that delivered hundreds of pelts abroad. At the same time a domestic trade that fed on the traditional interest in body parts for medicine further encouraged the hunters. There was a perfect storm of reasons to kill tigers, and the pest was rid from the land, probably by the mid-1990s in all four of the South China tiger base provinces, according to conservationists who went out searching for the last of them.

The tiger won't be coming back to Hong Kong. Not the true wild animal that used to visit. There are schemes to bring the subspecies back from the small gene-pool of remaining captives, but they'll never be the same thing. At best they will be happy captives living in luxury in a large and closely guarded theme park. They will never be the free and hungry beast of the forest and mountain that once wandered wherever its instincts drove, and regularly strayed into Hong Kong.

You can visit the grave of Ernest Goucher at Happy Valley Cemetery and read the final words on the tombstone: 'Gone but not forgotten.' That is how I wanted to title this book – *The Last Tiger of Hong Kong: Gone but not forgotten*. But I can't do that, because the tigers of Hong Kong have been largely forgotten. And we can't actually say which one was the last.

So I hope you enjoy this book, *The Last Tigers of Hong Kong*, and together we can perhaps at least resurrect the memories of the Lord of the Hundred Beasts within the boundaries of this extraordinary territory.

A note on place names

The romanisation of Hong Kong village names wasn't always consistent in news reports of the years gone by, especially for smaller, lesser-known hamlets. It is not always clear what today's name is for a village that was written about in the earlier parts of the 20th century. I found that there were even different spellings of the same place in different reports. Some of the locations would have changed names afterwards, or have been absorbed into better-known districts. Added to that, newsprint more than 100 years old is not always clear, even when digitised for library records. Where a modern equivalent is absolutely certain, I have adopted the names we know today unless the previous name is also well-known; otherwise the place names remain as they appeared in the original source.

Here are some old place names that are sometimes still seen, and their modern equivalents:

Old form	Modern form
Amoy	Xiamen
Canton	Guangzhou
Fukien	Fujian
Kwangsi	Guangxi
Kwangtung	Guangdong
Lantao	Lantau
Lyemoon	Lei Yue Mun
Pakhoi	Beihai
Peking	Beijing
Sham Chun	Shenzhen
Shaukiwan	Shau Kei Wan
Shun Tak	Shunde
Taipo	Tai Po
Tsun Wan	Tsuen Wan
Un Long	Yuen Long
Victoria	Central District
Yaumati	Yau Ma Tei

A note on units

Throughout the text I have standardised on imperial units for distance and weight since that is what the vast majority of reports at the time used. Here are their equivalents in metric units:

1 inch	=	25.4 millimetres
1 foot	=	30.48 centimetres
1 yard	=	0.91 metres

1 mile = 1.61 kilometres

1 acre = 0.4 hectares

1 ounce = 28.35 grams

1 pound = 0.45 kilograms

1 stone = 6.35 kilograms

1 catty = 0.5 kilograms

Wherever the monetary unit $ is used it refers to the Hong Kong dollar unless otherwise stated.

What do you call a tiger?

We refer to the tiger many times over in this book. My favourite name is "Lord of the Hundred Beasts", as translated by China tiger researcher Chris Coggins. This title is also often reproduced as "King of the Hundred Beasts" in journals and articles. In addition "King of Cats", "King of the Jungle", and "King of the Forest" are well worn titles for the regal feline. Hong Kong newspapers sometimes had the habit of referring to the magnificent animal as simply "Stripes" so we've borrowed that on occasion too.

Chapter 1

TIGERS ALL AROUND

1900 – 1910

Hong Kong expands into tiger country

The fateful ninety-nine-year lease that expanded Hong Kong into little-known, wild and mysterious hill country began on paper in 1898, three years before the close of Britain's grandly ambitious, empire-grabbing Victorian era. Until then the area north of Boundary Street in Kowloon, and hundreds of islands surrounding Hong Kong Island were all part of Guangdong province, tiger country. Not that it would have made any difference to tigers one way or the other. They don't stop at imperial frontiers, taking note of treaties made by humans. But knowledge of their presence could be spread or stifled depending on where a border is drawn, and which side of that frontier they are stalking in.

News travelled slowly around the newly acquired hinterland and the Brits were at first not in any rush to take possession. Like the tigers, the 80,000 inhabitants of 423 villages had not been consulted about the treaty Britain signed in Peking, and naturally the new landlords were cautious about not wading in too gung-ho. There were no telephone lines, and there were very few roads, mostly a network of tracks linking one clan-cluster to another over rocky hill-country deemed to be ninety percent scrub and stone. Pirate and bandit attacks were frequent in the area, where one walled village had been besieged for three months by robbers just before the new treaty came into force. The people of the New Territories were used to fending for themselves and defending their land.

There was a battle-hardened, trained and organised militia always ready to meet unwelcome interlopers, whether four-legged or two-legged.

The date was set to raise the flag at Tai Po on 17th April, 1899. A British reconnaissance trip was organised on the 14th when a number of policemen escorted by local Hong Kong volunteers travelled into clan territory and were greeted by unfriendly, uniformed men and a wall of pointing artillery. Taking no chances the British contingent made a calm retreat, only to return two days later with reinforcements armed with Maxim machine guns, and naval support out at sea from a gunboat called HMS *Fame*. It was after all the era of gunboat diplomacy, the great oxymoron, and the idea of avoiding a gung-ho takeover was instantly forgotten. Historian Frank Welsh informs us that "some Chinese" were killed and wounded, there were no British casualties and the flag was hoisted on 16th April.

Unfazed by local hostility, the British commander, Captain Berger, felt he was in a place that was good for the soul. He wrote "after the basely material life one continuously sees in Hong Kong, it was certainly a treat to find oneself among purely natural people where a man would not actually die if he had forgotten to put a flower in his coat, or to curl the ends of his moustache."

The "purely natural" people came back at the Brits in a force of 3,000 on the 17th, a day after the flag-raising, but their locally forged crossbows, firearms, crackers and gongs were no match for recoil-operated guns capable of firing 600 rounds per minute. They were easily repulsed leaving "several hundred" casualties. A flippant colonialist noted that "the gravest injury to the British forces was caused by an enraged and patriotic buffalo."

Taking no chances with his new charge, the boss of Britain's latest expansion, James Stewart Lockhart, quickly took the opportunity to establish his authority when three inhabitants were murdered. He burned down the houses of the suspects.

Police posts were built, roads laid, and telephone lines erected. Some kind of peace-like equilibrium was somehow imposed. News from the

New Territories started to filter through, and with that came the first reports of tigers in the British crown colony of Hong Kong.

The bones of the beast

In the 20th century tigers were reported with fascination and enthusiasm from the beast's heartlands of Bengal, Burma, Indonesia and the Malay peninsula including Singapore. But when they surfaced in Hong Kong the stories were treated with scepticism. That was the pattern that started early in the century and would never be shaken off.

Yet as early as February 1901 a correspondent saw the remains of a tiger in the New Territories and confirmed what all the villagers already knew – that the tigers were there. Rumours reaching the city had enticed several hunting parties to go exploring the New Territories. Mr C.H. Gale was on one of these adventures when he came across the remains of a big cat.

"From what I saw of the bones, the animal must have been of fair size for this part of China," wrote Gale in a disappointingly glib, and short, report in the *China Mail*.

That was it.

Our first tiger confirmation of the century was dropped into the conversation as a slightly gossipy titbit that presumably should not excite the grown-ups too much. It was the first of more than 100 reports from within the Hong Kong boundary that would drip-feed through the colony up into the 1960s.

On the one hand, tigers were taken for granted at that time. People did not know that the species would be down to its last few thousand within a few decades, and that trying to save it would become a multinational multi-million-dollar industry. On the other hand, the species was also inherently exotic when they appeared in India, Burma or Malaya. Yet for some reason, in Hong Kong their appearances seemed either humdrum or suspect. To be fair, perhaps seeing a few bones in the New Territories doesn't compare with the tales of ferocious attacks, daring hunts and sheer spectacle that were regularly reported from neighbouring lands in the early decades of the 20th century.

Gladiators vs potshots

In Indonesia there were gladiator-like man versus tiger shows for entertainment. On one occasion huge crowds turned out to watch twelve tigers battle against hundreds of flimsily armed men. The tiger-fighters entered the arena and formed a square around cages, the *Hong Kong Telegraph* reported from Java on 6th March 1900. The beasts were let out two at a time and prodded and stoned until they made an enraged charge at the line of humans holding up a wall of spears.

Twice, plucky felines broke through the spearmen and caused panic, but they were chased down and demolished. The blood sport lasted three quarters of an hour. "All the tigers fell in the unequal contest," the paper concludes without commenting on whether there were any human casualties. Not surprisingly, the Javan tiger was one of the first tiger species to be declared extinct later in the century.

The South China tiger was not to last much longer either, but in the first half of the 20th century there were still thousands of them in the southern provinces of China. Hongkongers regularly got news from around the trading posts in the region. It wasn't that tigers chose those spots, it was that foreign correspondents were there for other reasons, such as trade, economy and politics, and they just kept coming across good tiger yarns on their beat. The tales that emerged were numerous and consistent, including marauding livestock thieves and terror-inducing man-eaters. Every now and then 'Big White Hunters,' gun enthusiasts and have-a-go heroes from Hong Kong made the trip to Guangdong and Fujian to stalk the Lord of the Hundred Beasts. Had they been patient, they could have got one in Hong Kong.

In September 1902, a farmer from a village called Chin Wan found three of his cows dead. Determined to catch the culprit he sat up all night to keep watch. He got more than he bargained for on his lonely vigil when two tigers appeared, crawling around looking for their prey. He

*He got more than he bargained for on his
lonely vigil when two tigers appeared*

took a pot-shot or two, but he failed to down either of them. The farmer recovered some of his loss by selling off the flesh of his dead cows at the local market.

The newspaper made a call out to its readership, "here is a chance for our local sports to take a trip to the place indicated to get rid of the undesirable intruders." But our first confirmed bag on Hong Kong territory was still 13 years away.

District of man-eaters

The Hong Kong farmer should have considered himself lucky to have survived. Although it doesn't seem that many people in Hong Kong were killed by tigers, the man-eaters were out there in neighbouring provinces stalking people right into the middle of the century. Less than two months before the New Territories farmer's three-cow loss, there was a large beast over the border roaming around the village of Tak Hing on the West River, killing people and traumatising the living.

A missionary made a heartfelt appeal to Hong Kong readers, asking them to come up and shoot the animal. One plucky reader responded, perhaps seeking glory, perhaps hoping to help his fellow man. Either way he was drawn to the great task with the best of intentions, only to return empty handed.

It sounded like a chaotic hunt: "The tiger while waiting for this man to shoot him managed to eat a Chinaman within two hundred yards from where the hunter was keeping his vigil. The tiger is described as a very large one and has eaten over a dozen men this summer."

There was a close call in Hong Kong a couple of years later when a badly wounded man was brought into Tai Po. He had been working in a field at Au Tau, in Yuen Long district, when a tiger suddenly appeared and sprang on him, "severely mauling him about the shoulders, back and arms." His life was probably saved by his brave workmates who beat the beast back into a retreat. He was eventually taken to the Government Civil Hospital, while a party of "enthusiastic sportsmen" went on another failed campaign to "secure his skin."

Winchester at full-cock

Tiger hunting is not easy. The animal is extremely sly and until it decides to charge, practically invisible. In a place called Koon Wui, Guangdong province, another hunter set off on a trip in June 1904 that "though unsuccessful, afforded plenty of enjoyment and excitement."

Having got to the tiger-infested district, the hopeful adventurer haggled with locals for a dog, and headed up the hills to the tiger lair. He didn't need a particularly fine dog – no pedigree hunting hound was necessary, just a dumb mutt would do – as its sole purpose was to be tiger bait.

He also needed personnel, trackers and beaters, but he complained it wasn't easy to get local people to join his hunt, noting that "the Chinese stand in the greatest terror of the tiger, and even apply the propitiatory adjective 'venerable' to it." He did concede though that without effective weapons against the "formidable beast" the fear was justified. He managed to find one "sturdy yokel" and set off with him to spend the night in a deserted hut at the end of a narrow valley. The family that had previously occupied the isolated building had fled in fear of the Lord of the Hundred Beasts.

"I was not sorry then we reached the shelter of this hut," he wrote, "for the Chinaman with me had a nasty trick of looking over his shoulder at every bush and hillock which we passed. He evidently feared that the hunter might become the hunted, and, as it was pitch dark, this prospect was decidedly unalluring." They tied the dog up to its sacrificial post and installed themselves in their hideout. The hunter took watch from a loft window.

The marksman was extremely frustrated when the canny dog remained dead silent all night long, instead of howling in terror as it was supposed to. The canine obviously knew its life was in great danger, and only by keeping quiet would it have any chance of prolonging its life. It even held its mouth tightly shut when the would-be shooter could hear a tiger within 400 yards emitting a hunting whine, in search of prey.

"Thoroughly disgusted and feeling much inclined to slaughter the dog which has saved its skin by keeping silent," the intrepid adventurer and his sturdy yokel pushed on the next day, like the Don Quixote and Sancho Panza of southern China.

They met a party of woodcutters who pointed to a trail of spoors – tiger paw-prints. They followed the marks until they saw where the predator had laid down to rest, and put its claw marks in a pine tree. The hunting duo continued, following the fresh tracks, until they reached an area of dense jungle almost surrounded by hills to form a natural amphitheatre in a place traditionally known as an ancient abode of tigers.

Sancho climbed up onto a higher ridge and rolled stones down the walls of the dip in an effort to flush out a tiger as the Don waited "with a Winchester at full-cock."

Nothing happened.

Undeterred, the hunter followed a narrow trail and entered the thick jungle. The wild foliage closed right in on him and he ended up on his hands and knees until he found a "black and awesome cave" in the hillside. He hesitated for a moment, then shot blindly into the abyss.

"After some time I emerged from the jungle in a very dishevelled condition, and with no 'bag' to console me, but nevertheless the excitement and enjoyment had been considerable."

He was convinced that given enough time, it would be possible to get a tiger at that spot. Four had been killed the previous year and he urged like-minded adventurers to go there armed with a gun to "earn the gratitude of the neighbourhood by ridding it of some of these dangerous pests," like he hadn't.

Another hunt took place near Pakhoi a little while later. Two English men went looking for the King of the Forest with a pig and goat in tow. They returned humbled, minus pig and goat, admitting they took a shot at the King but missed. The villagers were said to be disappointed because they lived in terror of the beast.

Leave it to the yokels

Three female peanut harvesters, without the benefit of a Winchester, or anything like it, had a different story in the same area in July 1905. The women were up in the hills to gather a harvest and had set up a small hut to sleep overnight. They woke up to a sound they at first thought was a robber, only to find a tiger at the entrance. They flung themselves into a fierce and screaming attack with their defensive spears and brought down the 200-pound beast. Villagers heard the racket and ran up to the rescue with clubs and spears and finished the job off when they got there. They carted the corpse of the King of the Beasts off in a wheelbarrow and sold the meat at a market in Pakhoi.

And so the reports from the neighbourhood kept coming in.

In August 1905, Hong Kong sportsmen were encouraged to go after four tigers that lived in a cave near a place called Kai Kum Shan, north of Canton. Every afternoon the tigers descended from their lair and ate village dogs. The neighbourhood originally swarmed with dogs, but now there were only one or two left. The terrorised locals dared not leave their houses after 5pm. They had managed to persuade some soldiers to go and kill the big cats, but when the hapless troops actually saw the beasts, one of them was so terrified that he couldn't hold on to his gun. The others took that as an excuse to bring him back to the village and abandon the hunt. That is why besieged residents called for European braves to make the three-hour trip upriver from Canton.

A week later a party from Hong Kong, made up of Major Hatch, Lieutenant Maclean and Lieutenant Borton, along with Mr Sung Kok Pang and four Indians, took up the challenge. They camped overnight and at dawn stationed themselves at a narrow pass that they reckoned the tigers would have to come through. They waited there until they spotted three tigers.

But there was a problem.

The villagers had come out *en masse* to witness the sport. The tigers saw the crowd and sensed something was not right. Thus spooked they changed direction. After two more days of trying to sneak up on the stealthy felines, the hunting party decided to change tactics. They tied up a goat near the lair and waited. Once again the striped marauders remained invisible. The party returned empty-handed and a few days later a child was killed by the beasts.

Meanwhile in the same month, another tiger was killed over at Pakhoi by "peasants." The carcass was brought to town and "disposed of in the usual way," which presumably means chopped up and sold off at market.

Here come the Nimrods

It was a time of great change, and a time to stop taking old assumptions for granted. In 1905 Japan shocked the world by winning a war against Russia, a European imperial power. The two nations fought over tiger country: north-east China and the Korean peninsula. Manchuria was the territory of the formidable Siberian tiger, and tiger hunters were still active at that time in North Korea, tracking the big cat there.

At the other, warmer end of China, in Hong Kong, Sun Yat-sen, father of the nation, was plotting revolution against another old imperial power – the Qing dynasty. Taking shelter in the British colony, nationalists established bomb factories, collected arms, recruited troops and plotted coups in Canton and Kwangsi. Qing authorities were much perturbed by the *de facto* shelter that Hong Kong had become, and they attempted to extradite at least one of the leaders of the conspiracy to Canton on trumped-up charges of robbery.

Meanwhile, just across the Pearl River from Hong Kong, at a spot that perhaps is visible from Tiger Hill on Lantau on a clear day, ten people from one village, and twenty more in the surrounding area, were killed by tigers in early 1906. A district around a Hakka village about 40 miles from Macau, which was already suffering from a spate of robberies and a deadly outbreak of smallpox, became infested with a band of tigers. In another heartfelt appeal a writer urged Hongkongers to take up the gun and make the journey across the river to help these people. "Why cannot some of the Nimrods of Hong Kong inaugurate a great hunt and thus clear out these monsters?...it is a great shame that not more than 100 to 120 miles from Hong Kong within easy reach, these wild beasts are permitted to carry on their depredations."

Perhaps Frederick Lugard, governor of Hong Kong, could have helped. Apparently he was a bit of a nimrod himself. He arrived in 1907 after tours of duty in Afghanistan, Sudan and Burma, with a reputation as a big-game hunter. His favourite rifle was said to have been bought from the reward he earned for killing a man-eating tiger. Unfortunately we don't get to hear if he put the shooter to good use in or around the territory. Instead he spent energy on tussling with ministers of the Liberal government in London, who were morally outraged that the opium trade was still going on in Hong Kong. Lugard knew only too well that the drug provided a handy revenue stream and neither he nor his local administrators were ready to let London's qualms get in the way of good profit.

The formal meaning of "nimrod" is a skilled hunter, but in American slang it is used to mean an inept person. That ambiguity seems to suit the stories of hunters well, where breathtaking daring and ingenuity often travel side-by-side with unfathomably bad decision-making. One nimrod expedition in China met with success under circumstances that are difficult to imagine planning and voluntarily undertaking. A tigress was shot in a cave near Amoy.

Cave hunting in China

Edwin Pinches and his companion followed the instructions of local Chinese guides and spent a night at a mountain temple. At dawn they scoured the landscape and spotted a big cat making its way back from a night-hunt. They watched it enter a cave. Having checked the cave had no other exits, the braves tossed for the first shot, and sent their Chinese scouts in to locate the tiger. The fearless scouts returned unscathed to report that there was indeed a tigress and two cubs deep inside the cavern.

The nimrods silently entered in single file. At some points the passage became so narrow that they had to crawl through on hands and knees, pushing their rifles ahead. Faces down to the ground, they could see the footprints of the mother and cubs.

They spotted the tigress in a chamber that was about 10 feet square, just enough standing room for two big white hunters and two Chinese guides.

The feline matriarch attacked immediately, jumping for one of the shooters, and snuffing out torches in the commotion. The man who won the first-shot toss became the target of the tiger leap. He slipped in the split-second attack and dropped his rifle. His quick-reacting companion shot at the flying beast and brought it down.

"The situation was exciting, to say the least," Pinches wrote. He wasn't certain the tiger was dead, but could feel part of its body across his feet. The guides managed to re-light the torches and it became clear that the man who fell was severely mauled and bleeding badly.

The tiger was dead.

Pinches lived to tell the tale to an eager Hong Kong audience. They couldn't get enough of tiger yarns from the district and another big cat leapt from the pages of the Hong Kong press soon afterwards.

A fisherman at Shun Tak, not far from Hong Kong, spotted what he thought was a bundle of paddy stalks floating harmlessly on a waterway. For some reason he took a pole and prodded the pile, perhaps thinking the straw could be useful. The over-curious fisherman got a face-full of terror when a huge tiger exploded out of the water from underneath the bundle, and sprang to the shore.

Within a few seconds the ferocious aquatic beast had mauled five people on land and went on the run. Villagers armed with guns chased after it, killed it and sold off its flesh. It is no exaggeration to say a wild tiger is a terrifying, dangerous animal. But the Lord of the Hundred Beasts ought to know, and I suspect, does know, that as far as possible it is better not to mess with the Naked Ape.

Lusty screams of fright

People in Hong Kong got used to thinking that the district over the Shamchun River was "elsewhere". There lay tiger country, not here. But that was not how the tigers saw it. The British Crown Colony was within reach. It was a peripheral blip on the end of a vast tiger kingdom, but it was still attached to that land.

The tiger reports that made the Hong Kong press tended to be clustered around the few trading posts where foreign correspondents were stationed. It wasn't that tigers concentrated around Amoy, Canton and Pakhoi. It was because the vastness in between was a dark unknown, where a nation of farmers tilled the soil, and wild beasts stalked undetected by the outside world.

Tigers roamed everywhere around Fujian, Hunan, Jiangxi and Guangdong provinces. They didn't care about administrative boundaries, and they didn't do it for the benefit of foreign correspondents. In terms of communication, Hong Kong's nerve centre, at Victoria, across the harbour from the Kowloon peninsula, was probably better connected to the commercial stations of Pakhoi, Canton and Amoy than it was to the outer reaches of the New Territories in its own backyard. Those dark mountain tracks connecting the fields and the tiny clan-based hamlets beyond the tip of Kowloon were far away to officials, and reporters, in their normal habitat. Those trails over hilly bushland, pockets of lush greenery and through stream-gouged gullies, newly acquired by British administrators, were very much part of the Guangdong hinterland. They were in tiger country.

Yet just as much as tiger reports were sensational just over the border, the press often preferred to play the sceptic's card when the stories came from within. So despite news arriving of tigers all around the region, a hunting account from the New Territories in 1907 was delivered with a heavy dose of sarcasm. It started off saying "whether this story is true or whether it is a figment of the imagination of those sportsmen on the peninsula who see a tiger or leopard in every emaciated village pariah dog, must be left to the credulity of our readers." Journalists hate to be thought gullible, so it is sometimes easier for a correspondent to treat a story with scepticism than to investigate the murky facts.

The story goes on to describe how a party from the railway works at Kowloon set out in search of two tigers that had been spotted. The party found tracks, followed them, and caught sight of the pair. Inexplicably at this point the tigers turn into leopards.

"Our informant avers that he certainly killed one if not both of the leopards with his single shot, but failed to get the skins in proof of his prowess because the carcasses fell down a mountain 2,000 feet," our correspondent tells us. There are no 2,000-foot cliffs in Hong Kong that you can fall off. The story is amusing enough, but it is missing the wider context – that the tigers were there.

The Castle Peak tiger of 1907 to 1908 was dealt with more simply as a matter of fact. On 30th November 1907 the *China Mail* reported that a tiger had been seen roaming about Castle Peak Farm. The paper had a story that criticised a group of people who were planning to bring a leopard to a barren uninhabited island just so they could hunt it down and kill it. They were planning a pretend hunt.

"The man who wants to pit himself against the animal and slaughter it under the guise of sport should go into the wilds and tackle the beast in its own country," the writer asserts, before saying that there was an opportunity to do exactly that near Castle Peak.

A tiger in the area was roaming about "picking up the occasional pig, and the other day it carried off a cow." The gauntlet is laid for all: "the true sportsman who would have too much pride to corner a leopard on a small barren islet and pump lead into it from the shelter of a launch, is welcome to avail himself of a hunt in earnest."

Just over two months later there was a follow-up. The tiger had shown up again. It had stolen several pigs and two cows. But none of the intrepid hunters had got to it. Instead it was spotted by a grass-cutter who "fled with lusty screams of fright."

Educated Hongkongers knew that tigers were all around the region. But the grass-cutters, pig farmers and cow hands of the colony knew better than that. They knew that Hong Kong was well within tiger country. The tigers weren't next door, they were in the bloody backyard, and in the coming decades the weight of evidence would become undeniable.

Chapter 2

WHAT IS A TIGER?

The king of cats

Tigers, lions, panthers, leopards, lynxes, as well as domestic cats, are all members of the *felidae* family, the felines. All are cats of some sort or another. It looks like tigers and lions, the two most powerful and ferocious species of the family, have carved out different territories from each other on the planet, one predominantly African, the other Asian, but in the past their ranges overlapped. Today India is the only country where wild tigers could in theory still meet an isolated group of Asiatic lions, in Gujarat. But it is unlikely to happen, with their lands shredded by humans and separated by hundreds of miles from each other.

One big difference between the two top cats is that the lion is the only social feline group, except perhaps domestic cats, depending on your point of view. Lions live in prides, hunt and sleep together. They value family. Tigers, like most of the rest of the cat clan, are inherently anti-social. Many people swear that their domestic cats are sociable when they cosy up to them, but others are under the impression that they are just pretending. DNA researchers have found that the domestic cat shares 95% of its genes with wild tigers, so I would argue their domesticity is a thin 5% veneer at most.

The oldest tiger fossils were found in China's Gansu province and are believed to be two million years old. Genetic studies in the last ten years have shown that within the cat family, the tiger's closest relative is the snow leopard and the two species may have evolved from a common ancestor around 3.9 million years ago. That would suggest that when human ancestors started roaming Asian lands, they were learning to negotiate a world probably already ruled by tigers.

There are smaller tiger relatives that are often overlooked. The stunning clouded leopard is a Southeast Asian neighbour, more likely seen up in a tree than dominating the ground. To be fair, the fur hunters haven't overlooked this beauty; I've seen pelts for sale in villages on the border of China and Laos. Then there are the lynxes, the golden cats and the fishing cats.

In Hong Kong another wild relative lives on, furtively adapting to the intensifying density of human activity: the elusive leopard cat. When it is not being invisible, it is just as often mistaken for a feral domestic with a strikingly beautiful coat. I thought I saw one once lurking on a fish market waterfront, bolting up a tree with its bionic claws when it realised I had outed it. Another time one stared at me on a hill slope for a few seconds, then shot into the undergrowth without leaving a trace.

Generally it is the big cats that are held in awe by the clothes-wearing hairless apes, with species like cheetahs, panthers, leopards and jaguars representing some of the most admired mammals on the planet. Yet from this pantheon of select carnivores, the most respected, feared and storied are surely the tiger and the lion. And perhaps people could argue forever about which species is the true king of cats, but for me the tiger's astonishing stripes, hypnotic beauty and uncompromising individualism has to win out. In any case the tiger is the biggest big cat, so I think for the purposes of our story, we shall rule that the tiger is indeed the king of cats.

Tiger at the apex

Its Latin name is *panthera tigris* and historically nine subspecies have been recognised over a huge area of the Eurasian continent that stretched from Turkey in the west to Korea in the east, as far north as arctic Siberia and south to the island of Bali in Indonesia. It has lived and still lives in a huge variety of environments, ranging from the steam baths of Southeast Asian rain forests to the sparse and frigid forests of Siberia. Like macaques and wild boars, it is supremely adaptable, a robust survivor. However, although the tiger preys on those two species, it is now in danger of being wiped out in the wild before either of them go. The reason for that is of course us, the humans. We killed the tigers off in many places, beat back their territory and isolated their subspecies. Killing macaques and boars has not been so urgent to us.

The tiger is an apex predator. It rules wherever it lives. It eats meat, anything it can catch. Tigers don't like their greens, they are strictly carnivorous. Perhaps in their wild natural range there is only one animal that can stand up to tigers: elephants. Tigers must know that, as they generally leave the giants of the jungle alone. But the cunning predators are supreme opportunists and there is at least one account of a tiger attacking an elephant when the odds were in favour of the striped marauder.

An elephant in Malaysia had been hobbled by its keeper and let loose in high jungle grass to graze. The ropes around its feet gave it enough freedom to roam a grass field and satisfy its insatiable appetite, but prevented it from running, generally handicapping its movement. A tiger, or possibly two, saw the elephant, and must have understood the implications of the hobbles. It made the unusual step of attacking the pachyderm. Cries of distress and shrill trumpets were heard by villagers miles around. The flattened grass around an area of forty square yards gave evidence to what must have been a mighty struggle. The carcass was found with holes in its skin and neck, and a half severed ear. It looked like the attack came from both sides of the mighty herbivore and lethal fangs had been buried deep into the jugular. The skin was left like a tarpaulin covering the skeleton. The legs remained hobbled.

The only other species to give the King of Cats trouble is humans. One-to-one, and without man-made weapons, the tiger beats us hands down. The species ate humans for centuries. But we invented crossbows, spears, guns and traps, we got organised, and we got the better of them. We took over the apex and took revenge. That in itself was not enough; we pushed our nemesis to the brink. Then we blinked and realised we had gone too far. Now we are trying desperately to save our old foes and bring them back from the edge of oblivion.

It could be working. It helps that the species is magnificent. It is one of the charismatic animals. Its striking face and profile is often adopted as emblematic of endangered species in general. Some of their wildernesses appear secured for now, in India, Bangladesh and Siberia. The captive population has grown massively in China where breeding programmes provide questionable safari experiences and commercial products for questionable medicinal use. From an initial few hundred individuals some 15 years ago, the farmed population is now more than double the number of wild ones. Unlike the notoriously fragile pandas, these robust beasts breed anywhere. They can survive in practically any environment as long as they can get food and they don't get shot.

Many applaud the rise of the captive tiger. The gene pool is safe. But these breeds should not be mistaken for the real thing. A real wild tiger is intimately woven into its ecology. All its mighty grandeur, its cunning stealth and intelligence derives from its survival instincts in the wild. The tiger is only living out its full potential when it is pitting itself against us and its prey, not when it is being managed, sheltered and fed. The wild tiger does not wait for feeding time, it stalks us. Now there are programmes dotted around here and there that aim to teach captive-bred tigers to be wild, to be tigers again.

Man-eater

There is a persistent and admittedly attractive theory that tigers only become man-eaters when something in the natural order goes wrong. An injury handicaps them so they cannot run after deer, a disease weakens one of their senses. Or else they've been deprived of something they would normally prefer. Somehow there is a famine of sorts, perhaps naturally occurring, or quite likely something that our notorious species made happen. Either way the suggestion is that something occurred that went against the natural way of things, leading a tiger to turn its attention on us.

In India people believed the man-eaters always place their victims face down on the ground. They say the king of cats does this because it sees the image of god in human faces. It recognises the divine and it has shame, yet it still eats the victim, buttocks first. There is also a belief that it picks its victims carefully, preferring youth over age, and when it hunts women it goes for the most beautiful. Sometimes it stalks a specific target for weeks.

Once making the turn, the man-eater takes a liking for our flesh, so goes the traditional narrative. It becomes an addict of sweet, aromatic succulent human meat and begins a career of actively stalking the naked ape with all its cunning, stealth and explosive force. A man-eater is born. It is born because something went wrong. Maybe we did something bad. It is unnatural, maybe even evil. It is confusing.

There is another way of looking at it, one that I prefer. Like any animal, plant, organism, or life itself, the tiger is an opportunist. It will take whatever it can grab, whatever it can get away with. Like humans it is also intelligent and perhaps self-aware. Despite monstrous powers, it appears to be aware of its mortality. That makes it cautious. It uses stealth and cunning as much as supreme physical power.

With its intelligence it watches and learns. It studies the behaviour and habits of its prey, makes an assessment of their capabilities and weaknesses. Using that knowledge the King of Cats plots a course and stalks. If it doesn't think the conditions are advantageous, it will not go for the kill. It is the tiger's intelligence that saved humans in the balance, I believe.

Tigers watched us and learned. They saw that on the one hand we are spindly and easy to take out. On the other hand we can get organised, we come looking for the perpetrator, we will wipe out entire clans, we are dangerous. The naked ape should not be messed with. In the world of tigers, I would imagine that humans are taboo. Mother tiger will tell her kittens, "Don't mess with the hairless monkey. He is extremely dangerous."

Tiger observers have put forward the idea that man-eaters tend to be rare, and if a spate of killings takes place usually they are attributed to individual tigers. While the type of tiger hunts laid on for royals and noble men of leisure seemed indiscriminate, professionals were more often called out for hit-jobs on specific man-eaters that caused havoc in specific locations. This fit well with the traditional view of nature gone wrong. But it also fits with the idea of instinctive opportunists that are normally too cautious to go for people. What happens?

Rebellion, of course.

All pet owners know that animals have distinctive characters. Some dogs are more obedient than others, some more aggressive. They don't stop talking about it, the pet owners, the 'personality' of their animals. In the wild, tiger cubs have been known to grow up to independence and then snatch territory from their own mothers. There are tiger rebels. Some of them don't listen to their mums, and they decide to give the humans a try.

First kill – a thrill, but not as difficult as it was made out by the fuddy-duddies. Second kill, easier. Third kill and techniques emerge, the myth is busted, the rebel tiger becomes a monster.

But ultimately the mothers were right. We first went after the man-eaters, and then kept up an onslaught that wiped them out of much of their territory.

According to Gordon Grice, author of *The Book of Deadly Animals*, one survey found that 12,599 people had been killed by tigers in the 20th century. This is more than five times the number of people killed by all other carnivorous mammals put together. The Champawat tigress in India gained notoriety for her man-eating record, notching up 200 victims in India and 236 in Nepal before she was killed in 1907. Though the Champawat tigress is long gone, the deaths continue in places where the tiger still survives – most notably in the Sundarban wetlands that straddle India and Bangladesh, where several deaths a year continue to be registered by the species. Grice noticed that cats in general chase more often than they kill, and kill more often than they eat. There is an argument to be made that killing is something instinctive to the feline group. We know what domestic and feral cats are doing to the wild bird population.

Even the captives, without their wild survival skills, remain dangerous creatures. Records show that captive tigers kill their human managers and owners more often than captive lions do. Lions are sociable and they defer to hierarchy. Human trainers can create artificial societies for them, and place themselves at the apex. Tigers are unsociable and they accept no authority. There were 100 reported tiger attacks among the captive population in a recent fifteen-year period. Twenty-eight of them resulted in deaths.

Some believe that they are vengeful too. When Tatiana, a Siberian tiger at San Francisco zoo, was taunted by three leering men she did something she had never done before. She leapt over the 15-foot moat, and a 12-foot fence, out of her cage. She killed one of her mockers immediately, swatted another to the ground, and pinned the last one down to stare into his terrorised face. When police arrived she made a rush for them. It took five bullets in her chest and two in her head to bring her down and end her charge.

Before we get too outraged by tigers let's pause for a sobering thought. The World Health Organisation's annual report on road injuries concluded that 1.35 million people died in traffic accidents in 2016 alone, making them the leading cause of death of children and young adults that year. If you put that number against the twelve thousand recorded tiger deaths for a whole century, the big cat does not appear particularly dangerous.

The idea of a vengeful tiger does remain interesting though, because that implies intelligence, emotion and a sense of justice. We can identify with it because we are capable of vengeance. We grow up taking for granted that we are the only life-form that is capable of that, but when we step back and think about it, is it possible or even logical to assume that we are the only ones? Of course people resort to pseudo-religious insights to "explain" our vengeance and exceptionalism. Man is capable of vengeance and evil because he has a concept of right and wrong; it is an extension, possibly a psychotic and wrongly placed extension, but nevertheless an extension, of a concept of justice. Surely that is a higher thought, only achievable by a higher animal like man, and maybe, just maybe, a closely related primate such as the gorillas or the sex-mad bonobos.

Surely it is more rational to assume that every behaviour we have noted in ourselves must likely be possible in other animals. What if cats had a sense of justice? Would that not make us less exceptional?

John Vaillant wrote a book on the premise that tigers could deliberately enforce vengeance. "Imagine a creature that has the agility and appetite of the cat and the mass of an industrial refrigerator," he suggested to an interviewer. When a biologist was asked how high a tiger could jump, the answer came back "As high as it needs to". Such an animal is at the centre of Vaillant's tale about a Siberian hunter who shot and injured a tiger, stole food from the beast, and paid for it with his life. Vaillant believes that the big cat singled out its assailant, tracked him to his forest hut, trashed the place while he was away, and waited 48 hours for his return. When the man returned and found the destruction, the waiting tiger pounced, tore him apart and ate his carcass in a deliberate act of vengeance.

Vaillant's description of the crime scene is priceless:

"The temperature is below zero; here, the snow has been completely melted away. In the middle of this dark circle, presented like some kind of sacrificial offering, is a hand without an arm and a head without a face. Nearby is a long bone, a femur probably, that has been gnawed to a bloodless white.

They arrive at another melted spot; this time, a large oval. Here, amid the twigs and leaf litter, is all that remains of Vladimir Ilyich Markov. It looks at first like a heap of laundry until one sees the boots, luminous stubs of broken bone protruding from the tops, the tattered shirt with an arm still fitted to one of the sleeves."

Whether by hangings, decapitations, machine-gunning, bombing, poisoning or whipping to death, human history is peppered with such systematic annihilations of transgressors, wrong-doers and enemies. Yet we are shocked. Could the tiger really be as awful as man?

A tiger is a tiger

We have already seen that the tiger is the biggest cat. The biggest ones can weigh up to 660 pounds and be eight and a half feet long from tip to tail. Their back legs are longer than their front limbs, but the front paws are supremely powerful, embedded with the muscle bulk that is unleashed on prey of all sizes. The bones in the feet are tightly enmeshed in a tangle of ligaments that help to fine-tune bionic leaps into the air and the nimble landings of a densely weighted beast. Pads silence their stalking through forests and grasslands.

Their paws are armed with four-inch blades – four claws on each paw, and a dewclaw set further back on the foot that doesn't touch the ground when walking. This special claw serves as a grappling hook to hold onto victims and also comes in handy for climbing trees. The claws are retracted when the tiger is relaxed, carefully stowed to prevent unnecessary wear and tear. When muscles tense up in attack or defence, the ligaments tighten and the blades are unsheathed. The tiger can use those claws to climb trees, but it is only good at going up. Coming down is an awkward ordeal, back legs first, making the species a reluctant tree climber.

The skull of the tiger has evolved to cater for its other main weapon, a mouth full of slashing knives powered by bone-crushing jaws. It has a ridge at the top called a sagittal crest where the jaw muscles are anchored. Those enlarged muscles give the beast extra strength to clamp their mouths shut on struggling prey that could be as big as a water buffalo. They only have 30 teeth compared to a dog's 42, but with three-inch canines and back teeth that can shear meat off bone like carving knives, they are lethal enough. The canines are equipped with pressure-sensing nerves that help the predator find the best spot to slice through the neck of its victim. The small incisors at the front are sculpted to pick off scraps of meat, and pluck feathers off a bird, while the tongue is rough with tough backward-facing barbs to scrape the fur off a mammal.

The tiger's tail is about three feet long and it helps to balance the beast on the hunt as it twists and turns after a nimble target desperate to get away. It is also like a flag, communicating the mood of the animal, twitchy and nervy under stress, or relaxed and rested.

The stripes of the tiger are both on the skin and on the fur. Every tiger has a different pattern and despite William Blake's 'fearful symmetry,' the stripes on one side of the body do not perfectly match those on the other, though their faces are admittedly closer to symmetrical. Chinese people living close to the beast noted in awe the calligraphy on a tiger's forehead written in stripes meaning King or Lord. There are white tigers with blue eyes, and black or blue melanistic tigers have been reported but are very rare.

It appears that the King of Cats also has eyes at the back of its head. Or at least eyespots, like some species of fish and butterflies, to deceive its enemies and prey. Their white circular spots on the back of their ears make them look even more enormous than they already are, with gigantic wide faces when viewed from behind. They flash these false eyes forwards by partially flicking their ears inside-out when meeting a threat. This trick also appears to come in handy when bending low to drink water from a river or pond; perhaps at a moment when distracted by thirst the King can be temporarily vulnerable to a surprise attack.

All tigers are *panthera tigris*. Nine subspecies have been recognised in the past. The Siberian, *tigris altaica*, is the big one, most notably in the Russian Far East, and perhaps recovering a little these days with a population of some 400. The Caspian, *tigris virgata*, stretched through central Asia as far east as the Taklamakan Desert and as far west as Turkey only to disappear around 1970. The Bengal, *tigris tigris*, could be the most fabled thanks to the romantic and grandiose imaginations of British nobility in India, and the skills of their scribes. These form the largest group of surviving wild tigers, with an estimated population of 2,500.

The Indochinese, *tigris corbetti*, roams parts of Myanmar, Thailand and perhaps Vietnam. Its Latin name comes from Jim Corbett, a famed British hunter who killed the notorious and prolific man-eater dubbed the Champawat tigress. There are about 350 of these. Then, even as other subspecies were dying off, in 2004 the Malaysian wing of the Indochinese group split off and formed the Malayan tigers, dubbed *tigris jacksoni* in scientific language. DNA analysis had shown that the 250 to 340 tigers of Malaysia were distinct enough to merit subspecies status. The Sumatran tiger, *tigris sumatrae*, inhabits the lush forests of its namesake Indonesian island. There are less than 400 of these, the smallest of the tiger species. One reason for its relative smallness is that it lives in an environment abundant with food and so it requires less effort, less territory and less brute force to survive. This contrasts with the biggest tigers in Siberia that roam vast regions to survive in harsh spartan conditions. Still the Sumatran is big enough to emerge from the forest and kill a farmer every now and then.

Two other Indonesian subspecies were recognised: the Javan, *tigris sondaica*, and the Bali, *tigris balica*. Sadly the Javans probably died out in the 1970s, and the last recorded killing of a Balinese was a female shot on 27th September 1937.

The species featured in this story is the South China tiger, *tigris amoyensis*. It is a testament to the vastness of China that the South China tiger is in fact only one of five recognised subspecies to have been recorded in the country. The others are the Siberian, the Indochinese, the Bengal and the extinct Caspian. Yet the South China is considered to be *the* Chinese tiger and claims have been made that it is the earliest form of the species from which the others diverged – the original tiger. It is now considered one of the most endangered subspecies. That is the optimistic point of view that remains the official position of the Chinese government. "Functionally extinct" might be a more realistic assessment.

As sad as it may be to see the disappearance of a distinct subspecies of any animal, there are some biologists who see the problem differently. The disappearance of a tiger from any ecosystem is a local loss, every time caused directly by humans. The species has been hunted out of existence in Bali, Java, southern China and Central Asia, yet perhaps no subspecies has been lost. This comes from the view that a tiger is a tiger, *panthera tigris*. There are observable differences between the subspecies such as size and stripe patterns but those differences are extremely subtle and mostly invisible to the untrained eye. Compare that with the differences between dog breeds, from the magnificently shaggy-coated wolfhounds to the comically stunted forms of sausage dogs, or any other improbable pairs you might wish to pick as examples. The point is that these artificially inbred differences are all seen in the same species *canus lupus familiaris*. If you lost the sausage dog, you might lose some uniquely sausage-like characteristics for a while, but in theory you could breed it back into existence from the available gene-pool shared by all *canus lupus familiaris*. In fact you should be able to get it from *canus lupus,* the wolf, from which all dogs derive.

Over the past 200 years people have done a good job of separating and isolating the different tiger populations but there was a time when the boundaries of the so-called subspecies overlapped and there appears to be evidence of interbreeding. Today there are various tiger conservation programmes around the world and they are often seen as projects of national importance. There are programmes working to save Indonesia's tigers, or Indian tigers or Chinese tigers. As useful as that is for generating interest, political support and money, the national identity of the tiger could just be a bit of a non-sequitur. In 2017 the International Union for the Conservation of Nature reassigned their tiger subspecies to just two categories. The Sunda tiger is the new name of one of these, more commonly known as the Sumatran. All the other remaining populations have been grouped as the continental tigers.

The Chinese tiger

The tiger in China has always been revered, feared and held in awe. According to American researcher Chris Coggins, the South China tiger was called 'The Lord of the Hundred Beasts'. The Chinese character for 'king' (王), pronounced 'wang' in Mandarin, is even written on its forehead, a seal of authenticity stamped on by the gods. The vertically and horizontally symmetrical character links three parallel horizontal lines on a single axis, mediating and uniting heaven and earth. Babies still today wear tiger hats with the same seal of the 'Lord' to ensure good health and luck. Several Chinese minority groups have their own tiger traditions including ideas that deceased ancestors were reborn as tigers. There were tiger cults which taught that even the spirit of a living person could enter a tiger.

A tiger can inflict terror if it turns on a human community and in Chinese tradition that terror could have an ethical dimension. It could be a symptom of bad governance. There was a belief that if the rulers of the land were just, the tigers would be peaceful. To prevent attacks happening, officials were expected to offer prayers. As long as they were righteous enough their petitions to the gods had the power to make a rogue tiger leap into a cage, or get itself killed in a crossbow trap. When tigers attacked, it was the government's fault.

There was another idea that contradicts the concept of the man-eating tiger as a portent of bad governance. The tiger could in fact be a vector of justice, a striped avenger. If the tiger killed a hated landlord or corrupt official, it was obviously carrying out the work of the gods. Some people believed that tigers would pray for divine permission before setting out to hunt a human.

There was also a belief that the tiger could think rationally and therefore it should be held accountable for its crimes. Coggins who studied China's local records says that the animal was even put on trial for killing people.

American missionary Harry Caldwell saw in the early decades of the 20th century how much people feared and revered the beast. They attributed magic powers to the animal, believing it could disappear or change shape whenever it wanted. Part of Caldwell's self-appointed mission was to dispel superstition by killing the predator with his bullets, showing it was mortal and that it could be overcome. On one occasion when he killed one, the wise village elders examined the carcass and declared it was not a true tiger because it did not have the character for Lord on its forehead, and if it had been a true tiger it could not have been killed by Caldwell's bullets. Instead of three parallels, Caldwell's tiger only had two on its forehead. The scholars of the village conclusively pronounced that what lay before them was no tiger, but likely some metamorphosis of another animal, possibly a fish.

Harry's son John recalled growing up in Fujian province hearing stories about the "Lao hu" – a tiger that would eat up naughty boys and girls. Whenever his father successfully killed a tiger, villagers would rush to the scene with rags to mop up as much of the blood as they could. They would then attach these scraps to children's clothing to ward off evil and disease. Adults also carried tiger-blood swatches with them as they walked mountain paths in the belief that waving one in the face of an attacking dog would cause the cur to turn and run in terror.

Of course the elephant in the room when it comes to the relationship between China and the tiger is TCM – traditional Chinese medicine. It is reasonable to say that until recent decades, China's appetite for tiger parts was not a threat to the wildlife population. The tiger population was much higher, and the people who could afford rare TCM products were fewer. With a growing population of increasingly rich people in the market the impact of TCM takes on a different scale. In 1983 the official "Guide to Medicinal Animals of China" listed the benefits of tiger parts. Tiger-bone wine is a curative for rheumatism, weakness and paralysis. Whiskers can help with toothaches, eyeballs for epilepsy, and brain for laziness and pimples, while the tail works for other skin diseases. There are no prizes for guessing that tiger-penis soup is prescribed to treat male virility. Ultimately, ingesting a tiger tonic helps the patient do nothing less than reconnect with the cosmos.

Interestingly the skin of the tiger has traditionally had less commercial value than the parts used for medicine. The reason for this is that the skin is considered sacred and therefore limited in market value. It would become the property of the gods and often went to temples to be draped over a chair for a god to sit on. The skin of the second tiger killed in Hong Kong can still be seen today hanging over the altar at the Tin Hau temple in Stanley.

Tiger with a history

There were thousands of South China tigers for centuries, and humans kept a close eye on them. Chris Coggins studied 511 gazetteer records in the Ancient Books Collection of Fujian Normal University. These are reports that local officials were legally required to file on all important events in their jurisdictions. In southern China, tiger-related events were important, frequent and regular. Coggins notes that this collection focussing on Fujian, Jiangxi, Hunan and Guangdong provinces is the longest written chronological account of human-wildlife interactions in the world. It covers a 1,900-year period. The records also mention Asiatic black bears, wolves, red dogs, macaques, wild boar, rats and wild elephants, but the tiger appears more often than any other animal. Their reports are entered in a section called *shou zai*, meaning "bestial disasters". From these documents Coggins extrapolates a conservative estimate that at least 10,000 people were killed by tigers in southern China in 1,900 years, but he acknowledges that there are gaps, as nearly 400 of the reports do not provide casualty numbers.

The records show that attacks became more frequent in the second millennium, especially after 1300, and I wonder if that is at least partly to do with better reporting and the greater chance of newer documents surviving intact. Coggins links the rise of tiger-human conflicts to population growth, migration, social change and development through the centuries. There was undeniable degradation of habitat and there were demographic pressures in the second millennium that made more people come closer to the tigers than they had ever been before.

In particular there were large Han migrations to the south of the Yangzi River in the mid-1500s and more people moved into sparsely settled upland regions, disrupting local ecosystems and making wildlife encounters inevitable. The period of 1500 to the 1800s was a time of unprecedented environmental disturbance with mountain forests being cleared to make way for waves of human migrants. Of the 511 incidents recorded, 71 per cent of them were in that period.

Dehua county in Fujian in 1387 described an attack of "black tigers" that in broad daylight "ate people in their own homes. At night they pushed open doors and entered houses... crops were abandoned and returned to the wild." Some 500 years after this report, Harry Caldwell's son John recalled tiger infestations in the same province with the words: "crops were going untended; paralysis began to settle on the hills."

Notable for our Hong Kong story, Coggins reported that in the 15th century, as problems became increasingly common because of the human invasion of the marginal uplands: "Guangdong, as well, the estuaries of the Pearl River's deltaic plain... continued to record as many conflicts with tigers as did more remote mountain zones." Hong Kong of course lies at the mouth of the Pearl River, just off its deltaic plain.

One interesting point about tigers is that their robust powers let them adapt to environmental degradation differently to other more vulnerable animals. It is feared for example that wetland bird populations are crashing because of the relentless concreting of vital inter-tidal mudflats. And orangutans in Borneo are dying off as their pristine rainforest ecosystems are bulldozed to make way for sterile palm oil plantations. The tiger can adapt better to change.

While Hong Kong had famously been called a "barren rock" by the disgruntled British foreign secretary, Lord Palmerston, what Harry Caldwell noted in the 1910s was that deforestation was in fact a common problem all along the southern China coast. Wherever humans penetrated they stripped down the forest, harvesting wood for fuel. Much of the wildlife was forced to retreat to ever remoter mountain backwoods. Seeing this, Caldwell was puzzled by the tigers, thinking it strange that they would still appear so often on his missionary beat where villages were decimated by the marauders. The tigers would commandeer secluded ravines and caves to use as lairs and from there go raiding to "carry on their work of destruction."

"Black tigers" …in broad daylight "ate people in their own homes.
At night they pushed open doors and entered houses…"

This had been going on for at least 400 years in fact by the time Caldwell observed it. The gazetteer records show that human pressure on the Fujianese ecosystems by the 15th century had not caused a tiger population crash. Local folklore recognised the tiger's unperturbed propensity to stick around in deforested environments. They had it down that because the tiger is vain, it preferred not to tread the forests where it risked sullying its coat with bird droppings.

But another reason tigers did not follow the treeline up the deforesting hillsides is that they did not need to. When a tiger cannot find a nice little muntjac, porcupine or pangolin to eat, it turns on anything convenient. Humans have a tendency to bring cows, pigs, dogs and chickens with them wherever they settle, and any of these were convenient meals for tigers. Pigs are probably even better for tigers than their undomesticated cousins the wild boars as they surely would not put up as much of a fight. To cap this, the tigers have a great backup: if the domesticated menagerie was depleted, they could always break a taboo and eat the people.

In 1495 tigers attacked in Xinghu county, Fujian. Hundreds of casualties were reported. "In the mountains all travel ceased." In 1659 in Tiaohua township, Fujian, over 100 people were eaten. "The fields were abandoned, and returned to the wild." Coggins notes that the reports were clustered and typically lasted in a certain location for months to a year. He takes this as further evidence that attacks on humans tended to be the work of certain individuals. In a figure that begins to close in on the record of the notorious Champawat tiger of India and Nepal, one man-eater in Fujian was credited with 250 kills.

In nearly a quarter of the records tigers entered human habitations, many of which were walled for security. This also fits with Caldwell's 20th century reports of tigers rushing into compounds and cottages to snatch pigs or children. And though it was considered unusual for the typically antisocial tiger, there were reports of groups besieging villages, also repeated in Caldwell's accounts.

Yet villagers were not helpless. They organised in groups armed with spears, gongs, bows and arrows and old guns to drive away the problem beasts. They tracked the beasts and laid traps including traditional crossbow traps. They had their sorcerers with their prayers and premonitions. A sorcerer could galvanise a crowd of frightened villagers to hunt a man-eater by convincing them the spirits would favour their odds – though true Daoists believed that the best thing to do with a tiger was to leave it alone.

Thus tigers were very much part of the fabric of life in southern China for centuries. They were feared, revered and mythologised. They showed themselves regularly, snatched livestock and people and paralysed villages for months at a time. The wise and the pious scratched their heads and made up stories to help people cope with the awesome presence of such a beast. They created folklore and laws of nature to help understand how to live with such a beautiful, awe-inspiring and yet monstrous neighbour. Life in southern China was simply, by default, a life amongst tigers. And Hong Kong, it has been noted, is in southern China.

Chapter 3

CHIMERAS AND SCEPTICS

1910 – 1914

Kowloon kangaroo

The decade that held the First World War in Europe was also a tumultuous one in China, heralded by the overthrow of the Qing dynasty and the establishment of a Republican government in Canton. In fact it was the beginning of a series of tumultuous decades that would completely transform the ancient tiger-harbouring civilisation into a modern nuclear-armed nation-state that lost its indigenous big cat predator.

News of the fall of the Qing was received with joy in Hong Kong where people celebrated with firecrackers, cheering and flag waving – "a method of madness most unusual to the Chinese" according to the tiger-killing governor Lugard.

Frank Welsh tells us that even the prostitutes announced they would donate to the Republican cause and encouraged extra business for patriotism. The mood of celebration, euphoria and pride spilled over in certain places into anti-foreign sentiment, looting and the obstructing of police. This was not something Lugard wanted on his watch so he sent the troops in to flog the perpetrators. He would not be the last ruler of the territory who acted on the impulse that summary state violence was an acceptable policy for civilised society.

Halfway through this period, Hong Kong's tigers became indisputable because one was slain within the territory, strapped to a pole and displayed for all to see at City Hall. The tiger had killed at least two people, both of them policemen. One was Indian, the other an Englishman.

Ernest Goucher was only 21 years old when the tiger mauled him. Three days later he died of his wounds and today you can see his gravestone in Happy Valley cemetery, clearly stating that it was a tiger that got him. About half an hour's steep walk up to Wanchai Gap takes you to the stuffed head of the animal that is believed to have caused his death more than a hundred years ago. It is mounted on the wall of a cabinet in the police museum, looking unreal with plaster-cast teeth and tongue, and threadbare fur.

Yet at the beginning of the decade stories about tigers were still treated as a joke, and quickly after the 1915 tragedy, the scepticism would return, as if Hong Kong's incredulous residents, at least the Europeans among them, were somehow immune to the reality that they lived on the fringe of tiger country.

Thus when a tiger in Kowloon was reported in June 1910 to have eaten children, little was made of it and just over a week later the *China Mail* published a patronising poem dismissing the claims.

"Was it a tiger panther cat or boar? No none of these the huntsman swore. Ah, now I have it, what think you? Twas a wicked Kowloon kangaroo."

The usual pattern continued, one where all the sophisticated people of society wanted to talk about tigers, but none wanted to look gullible. Elsewhere some wit dismissed talk of tigers as being equal to rumours of giant rats from Shanghai.

"Having exhausted everything that might have had the semblance of a foundation, the native mind now seemed to have turned to the ludicrous for its mental gymnastics."

But even vigilance against the "native mind" couldn't stop the insistent reports. I have estimated a possible 14 separate tiger appearances in the territory from 1910 to 1920. By separate I mean 14 different tigers. It is impossible to be sure that the same tiger was reported on more than once, but you can make reasonable assumptions based on the timing of one report after another, the locations cited, and references made to earlier sightings.

I found 90 articles in the *Hong Kong Telegraph*, *Hong Kong Daily Press* and *China Mail* from that period that referred to tigers in the territory. I also saw 18 stories in the archives of the *South China Morning Post* between the years of 1910 and 1920, including four reports on the death of Goucher and Singh and the shooting of the Sheung Shui tiger. My count of 14 separate tigers could look a bit arbitrary, but I am quite confident that it is a conservative estimate.

Sometimes what starts off as the sighting of a single animal turns into the presence of a mother and cubs, or a pair of tigers. Other times there would be no report for a few months, then one will start by saying someone had seen the 'Kowloon' or 'Sai Kung' or 'Peak' tiger again, suggesting there were more incidents than the press had time to investigate.

In the reports I have seen, there are two confirmed human deaths, rumours of several other unconfirmed human deaths, one confirmed tiger carcass, and another animal shooting right at the start of the decade that is full of confusion.

This confusing shooting involved British soldier Sergeant Devney, two British civilians by the names of Gast and Morphy, and two Chinese gentlemen who crossed the harbour from Hong Kong Island on a Saturday afternoon in June 1910 and traversed Kowloon by rickshaw before setting out to the New Territories proper. The trip "reminded the inexperienced hunters of going into the great unknown."

A letter to the *SCMP* the week before talked of tigers that were taking pigs, goats and watchdogs on a regular basis, leaving large footprints near pigsties and hen roosts. The writer, calling himself "Old Resident", suggested that local sportsmen placed in the right position would be able to bag one of these "voracious and dangerous brutes".

"It should surely be manifest by this time to even the weakest intellect, that tigers have unquestionably taken up their abode in the New Territories," wrote Old Resident, mentioning in addition that tigers should also be killed using strychnine on their prey, as was done in Malaya.

As Devney, Gast, Morphy and their Chinese team members headed to the deepest darkest New Territories a week later through its rocky scrub land, it is not clear if they knew exactly what they were going for.

An old man who had lived in Tai-hom village for 64 years – which puts his arrival at 1846 – told them that the beast could be expected any time between the hours of 2 and 5 in the morning. The hunting party took up position on a hillock just outside the village and waited.

Shortly before 3am, a large predator made its appearance. Two village dogs rushed at the intruder and the interloper turned on them. Devney raised his rifle and hit the beast in its neck and spine, making it leap 30 feet into the air before landing with its hind quarters paralysed. In its death struggles it dug a hole in the ground nearly three feet deep before Gast ended its agony with a single shot. The party looked at the dead predator and could not decide what it was. It did not have stripes but some still insisted it was a tiger. Others suggested panther, and still others puma, though we of course know that panthers and pumas are from the Americas. There was even a suggestion it was a bear. Our Tai-hom resident of 64 years pronounced it a wolf. It was 5 feet 1 inch in length without the tail, and stood at 3 feet.

We will never know what it was.

Kowloon baby eater

Another tiger report was dealt with a heavy dose of scepticism in the *Hong Kong Telegraph*. It originated with a teacher, a Chinese teacher, who advised a reporter to avoid being out late after dark. "There is a tiger in Kowloon," he wrote, "and there are men who say that he is old, very, and the older he is the more terrible."

The hack pressed for more details and the sarcasm starts to rise in his copy as the account gets more embellished, by the writer himself rather than the teacher. This tiger is "utterly corrupt of heart," we learn, and that "not merely content with pigs and goats for which of course he could make no payment, he added murder to his crime of robbery." Any pretence at treating the teacher's story with respect is thrown out of the window, and the author runs away with his own words, and the force of his own creative powers.

The tiger ate babies, he tells us, boys especially but girls if there was no other option. A reference is made to popular 19th-century Chinese rumours about Catholic missionaries setting up orphanages to steal babies, leaving stray kids scarce for the hungry tiger. So deprived of its target of choice, the beast was known to climb into pig sties and goat pens to satisfy its blood lust.

"Decidedly it was dangerous to be out late," he apparently concurs with the teacher's original warning, only to rip it to shreds with a wisecrack punchline.

"We, in no way desirous of becoming a meal for the local carnivora, decided to adopt a plan which we have never had anything to complain of when tried with these animals elsewhere. We left a saucer of milk on the verandah. This morning it was, as usual, quite empty."

No doubt he was pleased with himself as he filed his fine words of smug mirth, seemingly oblivious to the wildlife that stalked all around his beat.

Aberdeen prowler

A few weeks later, the tone in the *China Mail* was very different, concerning the first tiger report on the island of Hong Kong itself. The author acknowledged the stories that came from Kowloon-side earlier, noting "we hesitated to give them credence." But now we get an account from "absolutely reliable and unimpeachable sources." The tiger had crossed the water, to the domain of the most powerful European colonists, only a few miles from their impregnable upland Peak residences. This tiger was prowling around Aberdeen on the south side of the island.

It came so close to the informant in the story that he could have got it with an air rifle. But he didn't have one; instead he had a camera, though unfortunately that didn't yield results either as it took him too long to set

The tiger had crossed the water, to the domain of the most powerful European colonists, only a few miles from their upland Peak residences

it up and the creature slinked off into the thicket on the opposite side of the road.

Views on Hong Kong tigers at this time were tidal. They ebbed or flowed depending on the cycle. On this day the tide came flowing in and the author states "undoubtedly the animal was a species of tiger" and that it is believed that they are fairly common around southern China.

The 1911 Stanley tiger

The Aberdeen prowler was the first of many tigers to reach Hong Kong Island. The next was the 1911 Stanley tiger, arriving in March of that year. You need the year in the name because there would be another "Stanley tiger" to come, a more famous one during the murky Japanese occupation. By 1911 the wealthy residents of Hong Kong Island, even at the exclusive upper reaches of the Peak, were beginning to realise that wild tigers were not just confined to the anarchic badlands on the dark side of the harbour, but could reach them at the comfortable residences of the elite.

When three cows were killed on Hong Kong Island in March 1911, the incident was reported to the police, generating much excitement, and the question on everybody's mind was how the heck a predator capable of causing such destruction could reach Hong Kong Island. A few days later a tiger was seen, hiding in the jungles, they said, near Repulse Bay. It was also spotted near Bowen Road, the popular haven of tranquillity overlooking Central and Wanchai. The islanders' belief in the protective power of their deep-sea harbour moat was beginning to look misplaced.

Tiger swimming skills are about as little appreciated as wild boar aquatics. The porkers don't look built to float, they look like dense lumps of muscle and bristle that would sink in the water. Their stumpy trotters are hardly paddles. Yet good swimmers they are. When there is motive to reach new lands, these trotting heavyweights will enter the water and push through the surf. There are records of them repopulating Hong Kong's outer islands after years of absence. Once in the water they transform themselves into hairy torpedoes that cut through the waves like purpose-built marine mammals. After seeing that, it is easy to imagine tigers powering through the sea, and in their case it is not trotters that they have to use, they really do have paddles, big, flat, deadly paddles tipped with retractable blades.

The Stanley tiger must have been a really keen swimmer because on 17th March there was a report that it had appeared on Lamma Island at the village opposite Aberdeen. It is not clear if that would be today's Mo Tat Wan, Sok Kwu Wan or Lo Tik Wan, because these villages are all opposite Aberdeen across the Lamma channel. The tiger did plenty of damage on that side of the water, killing five cows belonging to one farmer.

After that the big cat must have taken another dip in the sea, as it reappeared at Stanley to scare the living daylights out of a villager who saw it making its way over a hill. She changed her mind about whatever she needed to do across the hillside that day and turned around immediately.

This restless beast was also a keen roamer on land. Towards the end of the month the "ferocious" tiger was spotted on Kennedy Road, and near Shek O where a cow was found with lacerations and a goat had gone missing. In May a "native" constable thought he saw it in Shau Kei Wan. But he wasn't too sure as it could have been a wolf, or possibly two wolves. He chased after it, or them, and took a shot thinking he got one in the hind legs, but the mystery beast or beasts disappeared.

In June the aquatic feline paddled over to Lantau Island and left a trail of destruction there. Two cows were killed in Mui Wo before the roaming beast headed west and killed two bullocks at Shek Pik. It was clearly a very restless soul as it reached Tung Chung and Tai O on the other extremes of the island, killing cattle there too. In total at least 20 cows were slaughtered by the Stanley tiger on Lantau. In most cases the back legs had been torn off, leaving a gruesome and unmistakable calling card.

A group of intrepid hunters organised themselves into an armed human chain to scour the island from end to end in a bid to flush out the destructive monster. But it was not an easy call on the rugged and mountainous island with its pockets of dense foliage, deep gullies and steep rocky outcrops. The beast slipped through the chain almost undetected, though one hunter said that they had seen "traces of the striped gentleman."

In August he went to the New Territories, to Shek Yui, to maul a bullock before returning to Stanley at the end of the year. The name Stanley tiger might not be adequate, and it might be simpler just to call it the 1911 tiger. But Stanley is where it first appeared and where it finally disappeared, and it was significant that he got to the south side of Hong Kong Island, so we'll keep it. It was last seen by a Chinese policeman who gave chase without success, and its last recorded criminal act was to steal a pig.

Tiger stories dropped off in the territory for several months after that until one leapt from a bank onto the road near Deep Water Bay golf course before diving into brushwood on the other side. A gentleman by the name of Mr Eldridge had time to level his rifle and fire shots at the animal. It might have been the reports of missing livestock that had prompted Mr Eldridge to carry his gun as he went about his business. It did not do much good however, as the prowler disappeared into the bush with a threatening growl and no carcass was discovered.

Then tiger news went quiet until a thief made off with a pig in Sai Kung in August 1912, and a month later at 9:45pm an Indian police sergeant fired two shots at a big cat at Tai Tam Tuk, Hong Kong Island.

Mystery assassin in Hong Kong

Arguably a more exciting type of shooting took place in the colony that year when the new governor Francis May was the subject of an attempted assassination. Frank Welsh tells us though that it was all a matter of mistaken identity. The would-be assassin had believed May had been an official in South Africa when new laws made it difficult for "coolie" labour, mostly of southern China migrants, to be employed there. The law, they said, was the culmination of petitioning by activists who saw "coolie" trade as barely disguised slavery. The shooter, on the other hand, was said to be angry about the loss of his right to work. So he came all the way back to shoot an official he blamed for the change. But he was wrong, because May hadn't been in South Africa, he had been in Fiji.

It is quite an amusing story, especially if you dislike liberal interventions for the sake of human rights, but there is at least one alternative explanation for the attempted assassination. Another account says the shooter, Li Hung-hung, knew exactly what he was doing. May had previously been police superintendent in Hong Kong and in that role he had imprisoned Li's father as an undesirable immigrant. Li had a personal grudge that made him want to kill May. He failed, got caught and was sentenced to life imprisonment.

Tigers, in contrast, were not so easy to catch.

Another shooting incident in 1912 also probably helped eclipse tiger tales. Cheung Chau police station was raided by pirates, and three Indian constables were killed. The sea-bandits made off with firearms and about $1,000 in cash.

The official toe-hold on Hong Kong was in a precarious state of flux and power was not a monolithic force that blanketed an area within its borders. Power was more akin to the tentacles of an octopus, slithering up the communication arteries through patrol boat channels, railway tracks, newly sealed roads and forestry trails. There were gaps in between these lines where assassins could plot, pirates could shelter, and tigers could stalk and carry on their work.

This was a time when Hong Kong was still closely associated with opium, the wonder drug that brought the territory into British possession in the first place. When May came in as governor there was a £12 million stockpile that wasn't shifting. China was treaty-bound, thanks to the war they lost, to buy the stuff, but the post-Qing regime was determined to stamp out the trade. The leaders of the new republic protested loudly to the British, demanding an end to the enforced sale of the narcotic. They showed they meant business by executing 47 of their own people in Hunan who were smoking or producing the drug. Their cause captured the attention of British Liberal parliamentarians who made speeches in Parliament about debauchery and death from the powerful narcotic.

But the interests of Hong Kong barons were also represented in the House of Commons. Henry Keswick of the powerful East Asian trading house, Jardines, was an MP at the time and he told fellow parliamentarians that "It is no more an evil than the taking of a glass of beer or a glass of wine." What is more, he was strongly backed by big finance. Banks that had provided the funding for the £12 million stockpile were demanding to be paid back. With indignant British Liberal sentiment supporting the new Chinese government's refusal to buy the sullied goods, there was a solution that might please everybody – including private Chinese buyers eager to get hold of the stuff under the radar of their new Republican leaders. Thus the Hong Kong government became the monopoly buyer of the drug for the next 38 years, raising its opium profits from £1.2 million in 1912 to £8 million by 1918, by which time the narcotic provided 46% of government revenue.

Such a boost to the coffers was undoubtedly useful in consolidating control over the territory, but that did not affect the sneaky big cats who still seemed to know the mountain tracks and bush trails better than the civil servants from London. Brits often think of both opium politics and tiger tales as things of the 19th-century imperial past, but both of them lasted well into the 20th century. In the end the tiger outlived the official opium connection by about two decades, though the opium legacy in the form of heroin has had a more lasting impact.

The 1914 Peak tiger

When footprints were found somewhere between the poor districts of Yau Ma Tei and Shatin, discussions raged as to whether a tiger could hide in the bare hills of Hong Kong. The 1913 tiger obviously had enough hiding places because it would be spotted intermittently only to disappear again. Over a nine-day period it would be seen near Shatin, then Kowloon City, then back at Shatin again. One inspector O'Sullivan of Hung Hom said the spoors were very plainly those of a tiger and he had seen them himself. A gardener from Ma Tau Chung saw the beast and said it was a "tremendous" creature.

Then it was gone.

More than a year later the wealthiest residents of Hong Kong, far from the clanging discord of the Kowloon peninsula, had a new monstrous neighbour. He or she had footprints eight inches wide, and the unsettling habit of stalking muntjacs at night. His or her new address was The Peak, once the exclusive realm of the European colonial elite, far above the rat-infested and plague-ridden warrens of Kennedy Town, Sheung Wan and Wanchai. This beast was most certainly not a concoction of the ludicrous "native mind." It came with star witnesses, including the colony's Chief Justice William Rees-Davies, who had always been incredulous of tiger stories but was whole-heartedly converted after he examined its unmistakable footprints in his own garden. It is impressive how quickly a tiger sceptic can become a tiger expert when he lives at the right address.

Davies was one of many "respectable" people to report this posh roaming tiger that had a taste for the high life. Mr S.G. Newall of No. 5, The Peak, also told police he saw 40 footprints on the new road at the back of the tram station. It had crossed a patch of muddy soil near his house during the night.

Throughout March, April and May of 1914 the beast would be spotted. It even had a plaster cast footprint taken and displayed in the shop window of Lane Crawford. Many people reported close encounters, including a group of soldiers at Pok Fu Lam, a ten-year-old expat girl who threw stones at it on Mount Gough, and the interpreter of the Supreme Court, Mr Wong Kong-tin, who reported the feline at the junction of Robinson and Park Roads. It passed by a group of Western day trippers on a forestry track near Aberdeen, and although none of the Europeans saw it themselves, they conceded that their "coolies" had definitely seen something that frightened them. A bullock was killed at Cape D'Aguilar near Shek O. It was dragged 40 yards and devoured until there was nothing left except its bones. The Variety Exchange Film Company even had plans to make a comic film on the subject of the Peak tiger, though sadly we don't know what came of that.

Today in Hong Kong you can see wild boar that have become so used to people that they are almost tame. Is it possible for tigers to do the same? We see that to a certain extent in the tiger temples of Thailand and in some safari parks, so it must be at least theoretically possible. The Peak tiger seemed quite relaxed on human streets. Two European chaps walking in Pok Fu Lam saw "Stripes" close to Bisney Villa. They watched for quite some time as the beast stretched itself out on the road and sun-bathed. Around the same time, the sister of Mr Carvalho of No. 1 May Road saw the big cat passing by and several other people reported it around the Peak one day, and then at Harlech Road another day.

Inevitably the guns came out.

A hunting party made up of 50 soldiers, with 12 guns between them, set out at 2:30pm on 25th April 1914 to kill the lurking wild beast. After all the sightings they must have thought it would be easy, and yet the slippery feline eluded all armed men.

Tension must have been rising as rumours circulated that a "coolie" had been taken and partly devoured. As the police never officially received a report of the death, this incident has not gone down in history as the first person to be killed by a tiger inside of Hong Kong territory. It seems impossible to verify, but given that tigers were around, and knowing what they were doing to people just over the border, it is quite likely that people died in tiger attacks that were never reported to the authorities. There was a communication gap between the colonial masters living comfortably aloof in their luxurious compounds, and the subjects of the land, the tillers of the soil, down at tiger ground-zero.

That is why the Peak tiger was unusual; it bypassed the pig-farmers and the grass-cutters and revealed itself directly to the top brass.

Yet another sighting by frightened servants at Bisney Villa triggered a chase by intrepid Europeans who tracked the animal through bush and hill to no avail. Then a gentleman called Wong Kau offered to bring a tiger trap from China to catch it alive, and this story is beginning to resemble the saga of Pui-Pui, the crocodile that thrilled Hongkongers for weeks a century later when the mainland farm escapee set up residence in the Yuen Long creek. Back in 1914 the authorities were grateful to the would-be tiger catcher and said they would offer every assistance necessary, but the tight-fisted bean-counting bureaucrats bafflingly refused to guarantee a financial reward for the effort, despite the government's profits from its lucrative opium monopoly.

So Stripes continued to haunt the neighbourhood. It roared six times on Mount Gough at 8:30pm on a Friday, then shone its eyes through the dark at a group of frightened men on the junction of Lyttelton Road and Robinson Road.

Eventually tiger fatigue kicked in and the rationalists and doubting-Thomases gained the platform. A *South China Morning Post* columnist said that Hong Kong was "making a bold bid for fame as a colony of extraordinary happenings" and said that the tiger story was as old as the colony itself. He also said that "somewhat tired of the tiger" the colony had discovered seals near Cheung Chau. The writer then reminded his readers that not so long ago there were reports of a sea serpent, with pictures in a magazine, and the people "bored to death with pirates were indulging in the luxury of crocodiles and alligators." Once again Pui-Pui is anticipated 100 years ahead of time.

But of course, with so many star witnesses the 1914 Peak tiger could not be dismissed. Instead they tried to explain it away. One story that made the rounds was of a Chinese gentleman who had kept two tiger cubs as pets. Once they grew bigger he realised that he couldn't look after them, so he released them up in the hills. In support of this story someone recalled seeing two tiger cubs for sale at Central Market around 1911 or 1912.

Such a story could explain why the tiger was apparently comfortable around people. It is not implausible that this is what happened but when you look at the reports that kept surfacing throughout the era, the pet theory doesn't seem any more likely than a wild tiger simply turning up. And in any case, if two tiger cubs were for sale in Central, presumably there was a mother around somewhere in the wild. Similar theories would surface later about the 1942 Stanley tiger – the last tiger shot in Hong Kong.

Either way the reports kept on coming in.

7th May, Hatton Road; 11th May, Barker Road. Now the *China Mail*, backtracking from earlier factual reports, editorialises that "speculation is again rife as to the existence or otherwise of a tiger in the colony". It makes you wonder if the paper had got a new editor, fresh off the boat and who had not read back at previous reports. The story gained traction through the region with the *Malay Mail*, quite accustomed to reporting on their own real-life man-eaters, casting an arched eyebrow over this Hong Kong "tiger" that hasn't killed anyone and yet is "seen" regularly. Then a man at Magazine Gap Road said he saw a large white cat that wasn't quite as large as a chow, the so-called lion dog, and the *Hong Kong Telegraph* speculated on the tiger that became a cheetah, and then just a cat.

In May the police safeguarding the precious lives of Hongkongers finally shot a wild animal. It was not a tiger, though, it was a whale, in Tolo Harbour. They sailed up to the massive cetacean in a launch and fired three rounds into it. The whale took a deep dive and the marine nimrods didn't see where it rose. The incident was linked to the Peak tiger, as the police were said to have been embarrassed when the elusive feline had turned out to be nothing but a big dog. Presumably catching a whale would restore face. But they didn't catch it, they perhaps sank it, and even that could not be confirmed.

Over in Europe the First World War was cranking into action. German nationals in Hong Kong were interned and their businesses closed down. Some British volunteered, and Chinese workers were contracted as trench builders in battlefields. Dozens of Hong Kong expats volunteered for the Western Front, including Hong Kong policemen, but generally the colony wasn't greatly interrupted by the First World War. Life went on, tigers came and went, though any excitement caused by the beast was once again dwarfed by the crazy behaviour of the humans. 1914 saw the worst recorded case of piracy on the Pearl River delta. A band of pirates attacked the *Tai On* river steamer and unleashed a torrent of violence that led to 200 deaths from shootings, in fire, or by drowning.

The Peak tiger was quiet for the rest of 1914 and perhaps everybody was feeling just a bit silly about all their previous sightings. But when a report surfaced from Shau Kei Wan in November, braves picked up their guns and rushed to the spot. It was a false alarm, though, and in fine racist form the *Hong Kong Telegraph* gladly reported that the heroes arriving at the spot found "nothing more savage than an Indian watchman." The hard-nosed reporter discovered that the tiger story had been made up by the watchman's son who did not want to go to school that day and used the tiger scare to shut the place down. No doubt everyone had a jolly good laugh about that, with no clue of the tragedy that awaited two policemen and their families within four months of that date.

Chapter 4

PROOF AT LAST

1915 – 1920

The man from Belph

Despite the ebb and flow of Hong Kong's cyclical beliefs, the territory's tiger history is carved in stone at the Happy Valley cemetery. Reading the gravestones of the European section there, you can find mysteries, tragedies and layers of history folded into the soil. There are rows of lives cut short in their teens, twenties and thirties: scores of young sailors who drowned, people who fell to accidents or just died suddenly. There are plague victims and cholera fatalities lying not far from those who fell to flu, burned to death, or were killed in typhoons. There are young mothers who died in childbirth, and tiny babies that never made it past their first few weeks.

The police toll in Hong Kong is marked on the gravestones that tell of shootings and frequent accidents. Included are officers who died in street shoot-outs and murders. One officer, Ralph Miller from Tiverton, Devon, was accidentally killed on 4th August 1914 aged 19, and we shall hear more about him later. Amongst these stone memorials to young lives that give a tantalising glimpse into a past that seems so distant and yet not so far away, there is a grave marked of a man who died as a result of a tiger attack.

Ernest Goucher was only 21 years old at the time of his death in 1915. Many of his contemporaries were being slaughtered on the green fields of France in the First World War while he was living out a gentler life in Hong Kong's New Territories, where his beat was quiet most of the time.

He came from Belph, Mansfield, described as being in Nottinghamshire on his gravestone, but today sitting inside Derbyshire. In any case not tiger country, more like the land of deer, badgers and weasels on the ground; kestrels, crows and magpies in the air; and black fields of coal underground.

Goucher's colleague Rutton Singh also died in the tiger attack. His death came more quickly. Being a Sikh, his ancestral home was more likely to be closer to tigers than Goucher's, though we don't know if he himself had ever lived in any other tiger country. He died at the scene, unlike Goucher who died in hospital four days after the attack. We do not hear too much about Singh. He was in the second hunting party that arrived after Goucher had been mauled.

Goucher had strayed a long way from home to be confronted by a South China tiger. His father was a gamekeeper to the Duke of Portland, owner of Welbeck Abbey near Worksop. In the same year that the young Goucher from Belph, on the outer edges of the estate, travelled to the sweltering sub-tropics of southern China, the Duke of Portland had an extremely famous visitor on the estate, whose name would later become synonymous with the start of the First World War.

Archduke Franz Ferdinand arrived at the estate our Goucher was born on, by train from Worksop in 1913, and stayed at the Abbey as the guest of the Duke, ten months before his death would trigger the "war to end all wars".

Strangely enough, the infamous assassination that set off the chain of events that cost millions of lives may never have happened if events at the Abbey had been slightly different. Out hunting on the estate, Ferdinand's double-barrelled gun discharged when a loader fell down, narrowly missing the heir to the Austro-Hungarian throne. No doubt Goucher the gamekeeper would have been mortified by the mishap. The son of that gamekeeper had already been in Hong Kong for eight months by the time of that errant gunshot. And an errant gunshot over there would change his life.

Goucher was stationed in Central district, where life must have been lively for a 19-year-old recruit, though of course it could just as well have been bewildering. He had a good reputation, with colleagues saying he was a keen and zealous officer.

As Archduke Ferdinand found out for himself, it seems that Goucher family members were never too far away from a gunshot mishap. Tragically, Ernest's young friend and colleague in the Hong Kong police, Ralph Miller, accidentally shot himself on duty, triggering the chain of events that led to Goucher's encounter with the Sheung Shui tiger.

The death of Miller had a deep effect on young Goucher, and he asked for a transfer out of the bustling chaos of Central district. Goucher ended up in far-off Sheung Shui, where the pace of life would have settled to a slow beat, and solitude was easier to find than company. In this far backwater, so different to the congested cosmopolitanism of the Hong Kong harbourfront, the gamekeeper's son found himself in an alien environment. His new beat was embedded in southern China with its thick layers of village history and folklore, and in its native ecology. His new beat was in tiger country.

The hunter and the hunted

Goucher was already on the search for the tiger in January 1915. A farmer at Ping Yuen village, near the frontier with China, reported that his pony had been eaten while it was tethered near the house. Goucher, no doubt familiar with deer hunts, pheasant shoots and fox hunts on the Welbeck Abbey estate, was soon on the scene in the New Territories, inspecting pug marks. He knew the beast was out there.

Two months later on 8th March news emerged that at least one villager, possibly two, near Sheung Shui had been killed by a tiger. A desperate local rushed to the police station at Sheung Shui and found Goucher there with his friend PC Hollands, a constable who was on leave from the city, visiting the outback.

Goucher took his shotgun. Hollands was armed with a revolver. The two European officers led a party of several Chinese equipped only with poles. They found pug marks and tracked the big cat near to the village of Lung Yeuk Tau where a group of children excitedly told them about the enormous beast they had seen. Indian constables armed with carbine rifles were on their way, so it was decided to wait for their arrival before making the next move.

However, according to the *Daily Press*, a Chinese member of the party, presumably one of the fellows armed only with a pole, got impatient and threw a lump of soil into the bushes provoking a fierce response.

Suddenly a tiger "the size of a China pony" exploded from the foliage and leapt at Goucher. The PC was by all accounts a hefty lad, standing six feet tall and weighing in at 15 stone, yet when the tiger hooked him in its claws, he was tossed about "like a shuttlecock."

Goucher fired his shotgun, slipped and fell over a bank into a paddy field. The tiger pounced on him again and though it was thought it had been hit by a bullet, it still managed to tear four holes into Goucher's back, gouge his shoulder, leave his arm crushed and broken in two places, and severely lacerate his loins, shredding one side of his body. Hollands fired, and managed to scare the beast off.

They rushed the badly injured man to Kowloon by train, then across the harbour in a launch to the Government Civil Hospital, where they put him in the care of Dr Smalley. At that time it was thought his life was not in danger. Hollands believed that Goucher's sheer bulk had saved his life.

Meanwhile the hunt continued up at Sheung Shui. Another officer, Donald Burlingham, and a young recruit called Martin arrived with the Indian constables. They searched for the dangerous fugitive with few clues to its whereabouts and even less luck. All along the furious tiger was watching them, and the humans had no idea that they were now the ones being stalked. The tiger could have got away with it if it had stayed hiding, as the hairless chimps had already concluded the hunt was going nowhere, and they were about to give up for the day. But something

Suddenly a tiger "the size of a China pony"
exploded from the foliage and leapt at Goucher

primal in the brain of the beast must have decided it was a fight to the death, so it made a decisive move.

One of the Indians, Rutton Singh, was the recipient of the tiger's vengeance. It sprang at him from behind and swiped him on the head with its massive paws before tearing into him on the ground. Singh had a fatal wound to his skull and his body and arms were sliced with deep cuts. Burlingham's party came onto the scene as the beast guarded the corpse that he had mauled "in a most ghastly manner."

Confronted by this contingent the belligerent but obviously injured feline suddenly had no more fight left, and the party dispatched it with "the discharge of several Winchesters and service rifles." History awarded Burlingham the shot that for the first time in Hong Kong brought down a tiger, though he reported that finishing off the big cat was nothing exciting.

There was a belief that another tiger was also at large, possibly a mate, they said, though these days we are not so convinced that tigers travel in mating pairs, and perhaps it was more likely that one was a mother and the other an offspring. In any case the belief was strong enough to set the nimrods off seeking glory in Hong Kong's tiger lands.

The carcass of the regal feline was loaded onto a train and shipped to Kowloon railway station where news travelled fast that the Lord of the Hundred Beasts had been felled in the territory. People rushed to the station to get a glimpse and the authorities got their tape measure out to record for posterity the dimensions of a killer monster.

Here the definitive image of the Hong Kong tiger was captured by photographer Mee Cheung. The beast trussed by its feet to a bamboo pole, held up by Chinese "coolies" in front of a row of European bosses. Burlingham is in the middle looking stern and proud. Rows of onlookers go back craning their necks to get into the shot. The picture soon became the subject of a copyright row when the photographer discovered that a rival shop had made copies of his picture and sold some 400 of them.

The agony and the fortitude

It was estimated to be a three-year-old in good condition, though there were numerous wounds on the head, body and legs. It was eight foot six and a half inches from nose to tail tip, and three foot four inches tall. Its paws were six by six inches and it weighed 289 pounds. Some self-appointed tiger experts called it an Indochinese, though the evidence we have seen would make it much more likely a South China, a differentiation that was little discussed in those days.

The trophy was brought to display at City Hall where thousands flocked and besieged the building in the hope of catching a glimpse of the creature that came to be described as a "man-eating tiger."

A fund was established to help the families of the killed Sikh policeman, and the injured Goucher. Prominent businessmen donated to the cause, including the celebrated Eurasian tycoon Mr Ho Tung who donated $350.

The initial assessment on Goucher in hospital was that it did not look as if his life was in danger. A few days after the attack Goucher was said to be recovering well from his wounds. But then things went downhill on the evening of 11th March, and he died at six o'clock in the morning on the 12th. The *Hong Kong Telegraph* reported that he was conscious to the end and he "bore his great agony with wonderful fortitude". His coffin was placed on a gun carriage and taken on a procession through Central.

It is tempting to ask if Goucher could have survived had antibiotics been available to him. The attack happened 13 years before Alexander Fleming accidentally discovered penicillin and about 27 years before the wonder drug became widely available and revolutionised medicine.

Ernest came to rest in section two at Happy Valley cemetery, close to the plot where his Devonshire friend Miller already lay under the ground. While death by tiger appears dramatic, and Miller's passing sadly tragic, to die on duty in the Hong Kong police force at that time wasn't a particularly rare event. In the company of many youths and veterans buried in the soil of Happy Valley in the early 20th century, Goucher and

Miller would be joined in a few years by Sergeant Henry Goscombe who "fought the good fight" at the 1918 Gresson Street siege, and Sergeant Glendinning who was killed by a colleague in the isolated sea-battered marine police station at Tai O also in 1918.

Goucher's grave was marked with his potted history, in loving memory of "a native of Belph, Mansfield, Notts. Constable Hong Kong Police who while on duty in the New Territory was mauled by a tiger and died of his wounds on 12th March 1915 aged 21 years. Erected by his comrades as a mark of esteem. Gone but not forgotten."

Faith in tigers

An editorial in the *Hong Kong Telegraph* the day after the tiger killing proclaimed that the drama of the previous day finally provided a definitive answer for the sceptics who jeered at the idea of a tiger in Hong Kong.

"Why tigers should not exist in that corner of South China known as the New Territory the unbelievers have never been able to show," it said, complaining that the belief that there were no tigers had been enforced on people "as final". The writer proposed that the non-believers should now go out looking for the "mate" of the tiger that was killed.

The gruesome reality of the Sheung Shui tiger was seen as vindication for the alarm that spread the year before about the Peak tiger.

"Tigers are strong swimmers and a brute as powerful as the one which now lies at the City Hall would certainly make little of swimming across the Harbour in search of food if the water were fresh; though how salt water might agree with his constitution is more than we are able to say."

However, despite the excitement of the slaying, tiger fatigue crept in quickly. One letter writer only two days after the event wrote about the deluge of tiger stories that suddenly started doing the rounds. People who had harboured old tales of encounters and scares were emboldened by the undeniable fact of the dead tiger, and took the opportunity to share their stories from the tiger lands of the British empire, mostly in India and Malaya.

"Until Monday evening, I was quite unaware that so many of my acquaintances had experienced anything so exciting as practically hand-to-hand contests with man-eating tigers, the peculiarities of which had never previously been recorded of course, they had been far too modest to refer to these happenings in ordinary times," the writer complained.

Old stories from Hong Kong were also uncovered. One writer recounted the days before the British acquisition of the New Territories when tiger sightings around Castle Peak were regular and sportsmen often went out hunting. Regular sightings near the Shenzhen River, the theft of pigs and the mauling of cattle were brought up.

Yet at the same time even the dead tiger was doubted by some to be a genuine wild animal, with someone recalling an escape from a menagerie, foreshadowing similar theories that would attach to the only other tiger that would be killed in the territory.

We just cannot help it.

We see a dead tiger right in front of our eyes, but that is not good enough. It doesn't prove anything, the sceptics say. After years of doubt and disbelief, an undeniable tiger lies for all to see at the City Hall. As long as that was there, it was hard to deny that a tiger had been killed in Hong Kong. But was it really a genuine wild tiger? Does that in itself prove the other tigers were genuine? It proved nothing to the people who were not paying attention to the frequent reports of roaming big cats all over the Crown Colony of Hong Kong.

Skin and head mystery

Today we are told on good authority that we can see the head of the tiger that killed Ernest Goucher at the police museum at Wanchai Gap. Yet the gap seems to be in the records. Of course the war disrupted so much in Hong Kong, including precious archives and historical documents. But even before the war there are small pieces of a jigsaw that do not seem to join up to form a coherent picture.

The day after Goucher had died it was reported that the skin of the cat was drying in the compound of Central police station in preparation for being sent "home" to be cured and properly stuffed. They said that even in its present condition the head was "magnificent" and it would look fine mounted. It was noted that there were numerous bullet holes in the skin, and one shot "probably the one which resulted in death" entered the centre of the forehead. This is an interesting detail, as the police museum head does not appear to show a hole in the skin. Of course the work of a good taxidermist perhaps might patch up such damage, but there is no sign at all, and there is no mention of a bullet to the brain of the beast, a piece of drama that might have stuck had it been remembered.

Ten years later, when excitement was gaining around another big cat prowling in the territory, a writer recalled the Sheung Shui tiger. "There is nothing improbable in their story of its presence there for those residents who were in the Colony few years ago will remember the body of the tiger shot by Mr D. Burlingham in the New Territories being carried in the streets."

He makes some interesting comments about the legacy of that body.

"There would appear to be a good deal of haziness in the minds of those who remember seeing the tiger which was actually shot in the New Territories as to what happened to it," the writer notes. One version had it that it was skinned and made into a rug and was either given to the governor at the time, Francis May, or else it was given to a museum. Another version claimed that the skin had been taken off the carcass badly and it had to be thrown away.

The reporter however believed they were all wrong. His story matches the report on 13th March that the skin was being prepared to be sent "home" to be stuffed, presumably meaning Britain. It never made it there though, as the Japanese ship it was carried on got torpedoed.

It could also be possible that the head was left behind, while the skin alone was sent back. But I am not sure about that as it seems unlikely you would stuff a headless tiger.

After this there is little more we hear of the carcass of the 1915 tiger. Goucher and the killing of the tiger are often referred back to in fresh reports, but there is no mention of a head or skin and where they might be.

In the course of researching for this book I contacted Dr Malcolm Peaker, a former Hong Kong biology department professor. I was hoping to see if it was possible to search academic papers for records of early tiger appearances. Unfortunately he said that couldn't be done. He told me that Geoffrey Herklots was the only member of the biology department before the war, and that all his notes had been lost in the occupation.

Neither did police records survive too well. As Japan invaded in December 1941, the Police HQ in Central came under artillery fire. Personnel had to be evacuated to the Gloucester Hotel. Along with lives lost, and property destroyed, history was also lost and burned to the ground. Following more than three years of brutal occupation, the police force had to be rebuilt from scratch from a nucleus of some 200 expat officers released from Stanley camp, and local and Indian police who had been ordered to remain in uniform during the occupation. No documentation from that time of mounted tigers, stuffed heads or splendid skins remains. Indeed considering how much would have had to be done after the war, I can't imagine that even the eminent biologist Herklots, who had been interned at Stanley, would have cared too much about the fate of a tiger trophy.

The connection with a tiger's head that hung at Police HQ on Hollywood Road appears to surface around the 1980s when the museum up at Wanchai Gap was opened. We know that there was a tiger's head on the wall at the HQ from at least the 1960s. At the museum, you can see a picture from that era, displayed alongside the head. Two officers stand in front of an elaborate and decorated doorway at the top of which the head is mounted to stare out at all who pass through. If it was the Sheung Shui tiger, had it survived there like that during the bombing and occupation while so much else was destroyed, or had it been preserved in storage?

Ultimately it doesn't matter if the tiger's head at Wanchai Gap really did belong to the wild animal that killed Rutton Singh and Ernest Goucher. We know that they were killed by a tiger, and that tiger was also killed.

What I'm interested in is the question that it could open up, if the head in the museum didn't belong to the 1915 Sheung Shui tiger. What other tiger was killed, stuffed and displayed in Hong Kong? How many tigers were killed in Hong Kong? How many people were killed by tigers in Hong Kong?

I don't think we have the full picture.

The 1916 Peak tiger

Naturally many people mistakenly took the Sheung Shui tiger to be the last of an ancient race of local tigers and therefore the end of the story. But that is not how zoologists saw it. They knew that there was no such thing as a Hong Kong tiger, and that in fact all the tiger sightings in the territory were of vagrant South China tigers, whose habitat Hong Kong sat in. They came and went before the Sheung Shui tiger, and they would come and go much longer after 1915 than many would realise.

Less than a year after the first successful tiger hunt of the territory, a man at Wong Ka Wai village near Castle Peak saw a tiger carrying off a pig at 1.00am on 28th January 1916. He fired two shots and missed, then the tiger disappeared. Later in the same year a lady cutting grass at Chuk Hung village near Sha Tau Kok saw a tiger eating a cow. Lee Po ran in horror as fast as her legs could take her and alerted the village. A hunting party came back to the site of carnage and only found a mutilated carcass.

Then it was back, the Peak tiger, two years after its stories had fizzled out. Was it the same animal? Were they all the same animal anyway? We cannot tell. All we know is that when posh people see tigers the word-count grows.

It started with a report from an Indian police constable. He was on Bowen Road near the Magazine nullah when he saw it, nearly fully grown, leaving big footprints that clearly showed its deadly claws. The police were satisfied with the accuracy of the report, being from one of their own, an expert from India no less, who had seen real tigers before. They made the link with the sensational beast of two summers earlier, and assumed that, as then, this one swam across the harbour looking for good food – and The Peak of course would have the best. Around the same time the elite stock riding the Peak Tram heard a distinct growl from the bushes that sent a shiver of terror down every high-class spine on the carriage.

A lady staying in the home of Mr and Mrs Duncan Clark at No. 165 The Peak, along with a Chinese gardener, got a big shock when she cast her posh gaze over to the tennis court one Monday morning. She was alerted by the bark of a muntjac and saw the diminutive ungulate break out into the open, sprinting for its life. Right behind it came Stripes, large and creeping swiftly through the grass, like a giant feline snake. On the same day a group of Western children were at the end of Barker Road, accompanied by their Chinese amahs. They heard rustling in the bushes and a ferocious roar. The amahs wasted no time moving the kids away from the monster lurking in the foliage.

A couple of days later and there is the fair-sized tiger again at Barker Road. It emerged from the bushes and crawled stealthily forward in the direction of muntjacs. The muntjacs, also known as barking deer, are little dwarf deer the size of small dogs. They have outlasted the tigers and still exist in all parts of Hong Kong, but reading the tiger reports you get the impression that there must have been a much larger population than what we have today, because they are spotted much less frequently these days.

"Any doubts as to the presence of a tiger on the Peak have now been removed…" exclaimed the *Hong Kong Daily Press*. Three days later the *Hong Kong Telegraph* joined in with "Yet another view, this time one which leaves absolutely no doubts as to his actual existence…" going on to comment on how some people had been treating the story as a joke. From the Peak it is only about a forty-five-minute hike down to Happy Valley cemetery where the body of PC Ernest Goucher rested below a stone inscribed with the words "Gone but not forgotten." You wonder if those readers the editors were reaching out to and struggling to convince had already forgotten what happened to Goucher. But of course his tiger got him in the far wild outlands of the New Territories, another world as far as the residents of the Peak were concerned.

The Peak populace, at least those who did not need convincing that a real tiger was present, were getting impatient. They vented and dispatched letters.

"Sir, it seems incredible that the party which is looking for the tiger (if there is such a party) is still unable to trace the trails of the beast," an authoritative man wrote. "Why was the sergeant who saw the animal yesterday not provided with a rifle?" he asks before offering a gem of advice. "I remember when I was in India, they used to employ native jungle-beaters with long poles in order to drive the beasts out of their hiding places. This should be done here!"

I wonder if the man had seen any native jungle-beaters in Hong Kong.

Another person helpfully suggested using a five-litre gasoline can to catch the big cat. With no qualms about the dignity of the King of the Jungle, this correspondent, who perhaps had never seen a tiger, suggests that you can cut the top of the can from corner to corner and bend the sharp edges inwards. You put the bait in the bottom to encourage the Lord of the Hundred Beasts to stick his head in and push into the slit. When he tries to pull his head out, the sharp edges will be sticking into his neck, trapping him there. He could of course still run around in a blind rage swatting everything in his way with his powerful club-like paws that are each armed with lethal blades, but he would look pretty silly doing so.

And that is the last we hear of the 1916 Peak tiger.

The Temple Tiger of Kowloon City

Having got a taste of upmarket life at the Peak, the tiger was obviously attracted to the golf club in Fanling. When a big cat was spotted lurking near the 8th green in 1918, Major Robertson, D.W. Tratman, E. Grist, Mr W.D. Kraft, and Mr Kerr, the caretaker of the links, set out with their guns and ammunition. They tracked the "beasts" – plural – to some bush and commanded their Chinese beaters to wade in and beat. This is where the colonial nimrods might have bemoaned the shortage of Indian jungle-beaters, because the local lads outright refused to carry out such an insane command. The hunters had to leave without a kill and the nearby villagers were left in a "state of excitement" with all the cattle kept tied up out of harm's way.

It might have been a good idea for the authorities to persevere until the danger had been cleared, but Governor Francis May had more pressing human problems on his mind around this period, such as law and order. As tigers quietly stalked the lanes and trails of the Hong Kong bush, gangsters engaged police on the busy streets in machine-gun battles.

The Siege of Gresson Street in 1918 left five policemen dead. This violent eruption came about when a hunt for robbers led to running gun battles on the streets of Wanchai. The suspects eventually holed up at No. 6 Gresson Street.

The five officers were killed in the final shoot-out when they tried to root the desperadoes out of the house. Three fugitives died and several bystanders were injured. May arrived on site to personally lead negotiations with the last besieged shooter. When all attempts failed to draw out the last man standing, the governor called in the garrison Royal Artillery and bombarded the house. Today the fallen police lie in Happy Valley cemetery near to Goucher, as do so many other officers killed in the line of duty in the wild days of pre-war Hong Kong.

Another violent incident rocked the Hong Kong police that year, on the remote outer edge of the colony at Tai O, Lantau Island. It happened at the Marine Police post on the tip of land known locally as Tiger Hill. An Indian officer who had been accused of theft took revenge on his English superior, Thomas Cecil Glendinning, by shooting him dead, taking his wife and child hostage and setting fire to the station. The trapped wife was forced to drop her child from a first-floor window into the arms of a Chinese officer before she managed to escape by climbing down the same route.

The enraged Sikh officer shot himself, leaving behind a mystery as to how his thought process led him to such terrible actions, and the physical marks of bullets in an iron window plate that can still be seen today at the restored heritage site.

Tigers left no permanent marks, but there were reports of varying degrees of conviction in each of the three remaining years of the decade. The Conduit Road tiger in February 1919 was a vague apparition being a "large animal closely resembling a tiger", but the Aberdeen tiger later in the year came with more certain credentials as it was reported by police constables Cameron and McEwan. The following year we get a sarcastic report on the "Tytam" tiger which scared the police badly the previous month but had now been caught. "It is nearly as big as a terrier pup," they said.

And like waiting for a bus on a frustrating day, you bide your time patiently, and five come along at once. The Pat Heung Valley tiger was characteristically destructive to farming livestock, and though it started as one, it quickly multiplied. Sergeant Ogg of Au Tau police station certainly believed that there were more than one. He said that cows were missing in several villages and carcasses had been found on hillsides. Then a witness at Fanling golf course reported two large adults with three cubs. An amused observer noted that the prospect of adding tiger hunting to a round of golf could attract more tourists from neighbouring settlements.

The Temple Tiger of Kowloon City gave worshippers a jolt in the winter of 1919. People knew there was something out there because that something had been helping itself to local poultry. A group of people were inside the temple when one of them glanced towards the doorway and saw a fully grown tiger looking in at them. At this point I wonder if any of the devout might have believed they were looking at the apparition of a god. Surely some of them wanted to prostrate themselves in front of the Lord of the Hundred Beasts. History teaches us, however, that the instinct to survive was stronger than any instinct to worship. The devout screamed for their lives and raised such a racket that the Lord slunk away uneasily and disappeared into the forest, tutting and shaking its massive shaggy head, all the while wondering why the naked ape was such an insane and unpredictable beast.

Chapter 5

THE ROARING TWENTIES

1920 – 1930

Wild beasts and lethal force

Intelligence from the New Territories was still a murky thing 20 years into Britain's acquisition of the clan-controlled network of ancient walled villages. One tiger would have spots, another would be grey, their forms were often vague, they would appear and disappear. Such reports drip-fed a colony struggling for existential stability in a troubled region where old orders were being overturned. The fact that the Chinese empire was crumbling did not equate to an embrace of the British authorities. The rulers of the land were always treated with suspicion, as were their enforcers, their lackeys and their messenger boys. There was very little love, and not much trust, and when there is no trust, information could just as well be disinformation, facts blend with smoke-screens, and big cats fade in and out of view.

On an April evening around dusk a strange and mysterious animal triggered a wave of fear, expectation and excitement. As if intentionally making its presence known, the creature sat itself on a hill overlooking Hok Yuen village, near Bailey's shipyard on Kowloon City Road. Some said it was a bear or a lion, and others insisted it was a kangaroo or an orangutan.

One man knew that bears, lions, kangaroos and orangutans were hardly likely to appear from nowhere. He was a Chinese draughtsman, with knowledge of the local fauna, and he knew what he was looking at.

It was obviously a tiger. As sly as you would expect, the big cat dissolved into the scrub before police, reporters or any European official arrived to corroborate the claim.

When the following day a ferocious wild predator appeared at another village called Chun Lung, the locals went after it with their local weapons and hunted it down, to the mighty cry of "hai-yah!" There was great rejoicing and people started calling the bear-lion-kangaroo-orangutan, the "beast that never was," because it wasn't a tiger, it was a wolf, according to the *Hong Kong Telegraph*. Some did point out however that Chun Lung was a fair distance from Hok Yuen, and it was still quite possible that they hadn't heard the last of "Stripes."

The authorities, meanwhile, had more pressing concerns than shape-shifting beasts that haunted the locals. A fishermen's strike caused big problems for the colonial leadership under Governor Francis May, especially as unionists were being sustained by left-wing sympathisers across the border. Striking fishermen were welcomed in Canton where they would receive food and shelter while dwindling food stocks piled pressure on Hong Kong's population. The strikers shared with tigers a disregard for a formal border that separated the mainland from its peripheral British pimple. May enacted a draconian emergency law, bypassing the legislative council, to impose a ban on those unionists freely stepping over the boundary into the mainland. When a group tried to ignore warnings and cross over regardless, five of them were gunned down by guards, instantly proving that tigers were not even close to being the most dangerous animal in the territory.

When it came to the question of risk of life posed by big cats in southern China, it was complicated. Humans definitely killed each other more than were killed by feline predators. Yet the imminent danger of a tiger was undeniable to those who lived cheek-by-jowl with big cats on the hillsides. The rural population of Guangdong province knew all about the man-eaters, the kid-snatchers and the night-prowlers. Every now and then the Big White Hunter got wind of some excitement across the border, such as a family of big cats occupying a cave and terrorising a village. "An opportunity for sportsmen," the papers would say and the big-city nimrods from Hong Kong side set off.

Once in the hunting ground the shooters would need to recruit locals and invariably they experienced the first of many frustrations. Not many Chinese natives wanted to volunteer for the frontline of the hunt. Hunting is not a sport if you need to survive with little protection in a land infested with tigers, as was the case for tens of thousands of people in the tiger heartlands of southern China. The incoming marksmen more often than not mistook this reluctance to join the sport as cowardice. Yet this was a misunderstanding about a people who had deep insights about their predators, and knew very well that the defence of life and property from the monster in the hills was a deadly serious pursuit, and not a sport. Indeed many ordinary people whose lives depended on the land, and who had no choice but to spend long periods of time isolated in the grasses and the woods, were extraordinarily brave in the presence of wild predators.

Tiger-lore mostly travelled under the radar of the white administrators of Victoria and Kowloon; it travelled among the amahs, the traders, the grass-cutters and the "coolie" labourers. While many a resident of the Peak scoffed at rumours of wild beasts prowling the country lanes, mothers and fathers in villages passed on South China wisdom to children, and taught them to be cautious and courageous in the face of danger. A court case in Hong Kong became the unexpected setting for an exchange that illustrated beautifully the separate and parallel universes that people occupied in the territory. This difference left them mutually baffled about each other's attitude towards wildlife.

At the centre of the case there was a man who died in a suspected poisoning. In the dock was his wife, accused of using the Ho Man Tung herb from the Lantau hillside to kill her husband. It was a well-known plant to be avoided by locals because even a sniff of it in the vicinity heated up the body and gave rise to dizzying nausea. The antidote was goat's blood, no doubt naturally enriched with antibodies accumulated by the indiscriminate muncher of the hills, a folkloric version of convalescent plasma therapy.

The dead man's mother was in the witness stand telling the court that whenever her daughter-in-law met her husband she turned up her eyes and treated him with contempt. But she was unable to say if she saw the prisoner cooking her husband's midday meal, the poisoned lunch that killed him.

Eminent lawyer Mr Campbell Prosser, cross-examining for the defence, wanted to know why the witness had missed this crucial piece of evidence. The accusing mother explained carefully that she often stayed in the fields instead of coming home for her midday meal because there was a tiger in the hills.

Prosser was baffled.

Why on earth would a helpless country-woman stay in the fields if there was a tiger at large?

She, in turn, was equally baffled by the lawyer's ignorance.

Naturally, if there is a tiger about, you stay close to your animals to guard them from the predator.

The incredulity of those who took ownership of Hong Kong contrasted with the practical and commonsensical folklore of the people who worked its land.

The court did not dwell on the tiger. Prosser went on to ask if the witness had broken an earthenware pot belonging to the prisoner, to which she replied, "there are many disputes and many quarrels but a mother-in-law does not break earthenware pots."

Tigers in the time of revolution

Sun Yat-sen, the father of the Chinese revolution and former Hong Kong University medical student, died in 1925. He left Canton in the hands of an uneasy alliance between his nationalist Kuomintang, and the up and coming Communists. Northern China was under warlords. It was a time of instability and violence, so when the Sha Tau Kok tiger appeared, there was an available explanation.

Just like the unionised fishermen before May's hail of bullets, the ferocious rambler seemed to strut back and forth over the boundary as if it wasn't there. That was not a difficult thing to do in a place where the border at that time was a small stream that would later dry up and become the main road in the village.

This raider of Hong Kong and China had killed at least six buffalo, scattering partly-eaten remains in various places, in both China and Hong Kong. Some plucky villagers had chased the marauder with bamboo poles and when they couldn't get it they asked the better-armed Hong Kong police to help out.

The general thinking was that the big cat had been driven down from the hills by the uncertainties of a land in turmoil, and the extensive movement of gun-toting troops vying for control. For exactly the same reason, deer were appearing in larger numbers than usual, adding to the incentive of the tigers to head south to the Crown Colony.

Once again the feline eluded capture by the uniformed troops, so one ambitious gunman who had had enough went out determined to get the beast alone. He used the kid-lure method, tying up a pair of goats, and then sought out a suitable high perch to wait in. Unfortunately, Hong Kong being still largely a barren rock, the shooter couldn't find the right tree so he had to make do with a mound of stones.

Harry Caldwell, the missionary tiger shooter of Fujian, would have made himself a hide among the bushes on the ground, but our man's instinct was to go high. It was high enough for the tiger to see him, as the irritated feline spent the whole night growling at the terrified hunter from the dark below, but never broke cover to reveal itself.

One week later, back in Sha Tau Kok, two more water buffaloes were attacked. But they were still alive when they were discovered, which suggests the tiger was nearby waiting for them to bleed out and die. The discoverers found them so badly mauled that they had to put them out of their misery. Once again a hunting party set out equipped with guns and sacrificial goats. They tied up the ruminants outside a hut and waited.

After a while it got monotonous, so they packed up their paraphernalia and made for home.

Caldwell would have told them, it takes great patience to hunt a tiger.

Tiger-spotting is a man's game

This was a time of constant crisis when strikers in 1925 were once again withdrawing their labour from the colony, bringing the place to a standstill. It wasn't even Hong Kong's fault, to start with. British imperial police in the Shanghai French quarter had shot eleven Chinese demonstrators, and anti-imperial sentiments had travelled south, with the full encouragement of mainland activists. When British-led troops at the foreign concession in Canton tried to calm the situation by shooting 52 demonstrators dead, a violent, anti-British fury ignited Hong Kong, which was now governed by Reginald Stubbs. A quarter of a million disgusted people left the colony to be welcomed once again by strike committees over the border, where they were housed, fed and clothed. The itinerant tigers must have been perturbed that the narrow neck that is the Hong Kong land border was a constant throng of activity, with humans not knowing whether they were coming or going.

Despite such wild swings of chaos at times in the roaring twenties, somehow the territory pulled back to regain a renewed platform of calm. The government threw opium money at the banks to help them ride out a run on accounts. The better-connected Chinese, especially those associated around the Tung Wah hospital, rallied for stability in the colony. Dark elements countered anti-imperialist intimidation with harder anti-anti-imperialist intimidation. A new normal began to establish. Labourers returned, the economy picked itself back up and Stubbs was replaced by Cecil Clementi, a fluent Cantonese-speaking Old China Hand who had been in the mainland at the time of the Boxer Rebellion.

While Clementi left his name on a trail on the north side of Hong Kong Island, his better half left her name on the bridleways and paths on the south side, on the remote tracks that stealthy tigers sometimes trod. Lady Clementi loved to ride her horse around those forest trails throughout what is now Aberdeen Country Park, the tracks where occasional tiger sightings on the island were reported, though there is no record of a sighting by her ladyship. From Wanchai Gap you can drop down Lady Clementi's Ride and connect with other trails on the south side, and eventually hit what in the 1920s were pristine golden beaches. Deep Water Bay comes first, then the splendid Repulse Bay, where the famous hotel was built in 1920.

Looking out from the vicinity of the Repulse Bay Hotel, just after Clementi had arrived to a peace-restored Hong Kong, two ladies noticed with alarm a scary-looking creature prowling up and down the beach. Word went out: tiger at large, but luckily there was a man about to check if the ladies had got it right. After all, fine ladies at the Repulse Bay Hotel may not be so familiar with the wildlife their menfolk had to tackle. Only white men had the ability to confirm tiger sightings in the 1920s.

Sure enough, the alarm was called off. Graciously the menfolk conceded that the women had seen a real creature, not just a phantom. But it was no tiger, it was only a harmless little deer. Perhaps the poor women had quaffed a bit too much gin that afternoon. And yet, in a matter of months respectable Hong Kong men as well as women would have the opportunity to see a real live tiger captured in the colony, on exhibit at Causeway Bay.

Some time later white men were able to confirm a different tiger sighting. Chinese farmers on the "dark side", across the harbour from the lovely Peak, insisted a tiger was on the prowl stealing pigs and poultry. The neighbourhoods of Kowloon City and Kowloon Tong were being prowled by the Lord of the Hundred Beasts. But the first reports only came from Chinese sources, so the Peak residents surely could not take them as fact. All was settled however on 19th December when a group of Europeans saw the big cat themselves, specifically when the menfolk confirmed it.

A party of three men and three women were rambling up Kowloon Peak. One of the ladies pushed ahead with the advance group until she suddenly came running back shouting the warning to get back, as they had seen a tiger. The women huddled for safety while the three men went ahead to investigate. They saw the big cat forty or fifty yards ahead, moving stealthily between the trees. It looked young, maybe not fully grown, five or six feet long. Its colouring was fawn or grey, with black stripes.

Live in Lee Garden

A hunter from Cheung Lak Mui, Shatin district, set a deer trap at Cheung Tam Hill, about 400 yards from his village. When he went back to check, the snare was missing but there were marks on the ground. He could see that a powerful beast had dragged the trap into the undergrowth. The hunter followed the trail to a deep pit and there came face to face with a snarling, growling tiger that was helplessly hobbled by the steel clamp on its broken leg.

Somehow the hunter managed to get the seething cat into a cage alive. It is pure luck that we know about this animal because the villagers did not then go to report the dangerous wildlife to the colonial authorities. Instead they headed down Tai Po Road with their exotic captive, towards the railway station, when a policeman came across the party by chance. The fact of another tiger having been caught in the New Territories might not have been known if it had not been for this lucky discovery, the *Hong Kong Telegraph* noted.

"Another" tiger? Was that a reference to the 1915 Sheung Shui tiger? That one was killed, which I suppose is the same as being caught, but a live tiger is a different entity to a dead tiger. Surely that wouldn't be just another tiger caught dead-or-alive, it would be the first live-caught. Were there other live tigers caught? It seems distinctly possible. If the opportunists of Cheung Lak Mui village had no intention of reporting the predator, wouldn't the people of other villages have had a similar attitude? Especially in a period when relations between Chinese inhabitants and colonial authorities were as rocky as we have seen. It was basic common sense in the New Territories to try and have as little

They headed down Tai Po Road with their exotic captive, towards the railway station, when a policeman came across the party by chance

to do with the authorities as possible, and that would have applied to
the wildlife trade as much as anything else. This attitude remained in the
territory for decades, and perhaps remains true today.

The *China Mail* noted that it had been some years since evidence had
been found to "confute the sceptical in the matter of the presence of
tigers." And the *Daily Press* said that reports of tigers had been made
often, but they were usually received sceptically. Now the press had a
reliable account from the police, and a living specimen for all to see.

We don't learn if the villagers got what they hoped for from the tiger,
or even what they were going to do with it. They were heading for the
railway station. Could they have been planning to sell it in China? Or
were they heading the other way, to Central Market, where the occasional
sale of tiger flesh and bones was rumoured? In any case the wild tiger
made it into the hands of the officials and the wealthy, and was briefly
exhibited on Hong Kong Island.

Lee Garden was budding tycoon Lee Hysan's first foothold in the
district known then as East Point, today's Causeway Bay. He opened
the Lee Garden Amusement Park in 1923 as a place of entertainment.
Today various properties around the original Lee Garden site are part of
a multimillion-dollar property portfolio that is arguably the commercial
epicentre of Causeway Bay and still owned by the Hysan group.

It was right there at the early toe-hold of the Hysan empire that a
wild-caught tiger was displayed to the people of Hong Kong, though it
did not last long and memories faded. After a short period of display it
was decided that the village-crafted cage was not adequate to hold the
wild animal. They shifted the captive to Yau Ma Tei police station while
a proper cage was commissioned. Sadly while still in police custody the
tiger succumbed to infection from festering wounds originally inflicted
by the snare.

We are told that the "owner" of the animal didn't want any parts of
the deceased as a trophy. It isn't clear who the owner was, but this seems
unusual. In other accounts of Chinese village reactions to dead tigers,
there is huge enthusiasm for harvesting many parts of the carcass that

hold great value for traditional medicine and folklore. But no one came forward to make the claim, so Sub-Inspector Hutchins of Yau Ma Tei police station became the proud possessor of the skin of a genuine Hong Kong tiger.

Slave-girls, houseboys, amahs and their tigers

Towards the end of the 1920s a great row was broiling about slave-girls in Hong Kong. The *mui tsai* system was the practice of poor families farming out their daughters to wealthy households where they would grow up to serve their benefactors. Conservative Chinese patriarchs defended the tradition saying that it helped desperate families, and provided stability to the 'little sisters'. Liberal British society, championed back home by Winston Churchill, focussed on the inevitable abuses that spun out of the practice, from torture and slavery to prostitution. Lady Clementi's husband was caught between opposing sides, but appeared to lean towards respectable Chinese society led by the newly formed Po Leung Kuk. The group ostensibly campaigned against acknowledged evil by-products of the system, but worked to preserve the tradition in what it regarded as its benevolent form. The colony muddled through the moral maze and created a registry, and the remnants of the practice rumbled on for a few more decades.

Houseboys on the Peak, on the other hand, were presumably treated always with respect and dignity by their entitled European masters, no matter what age the 'boy' was. One such servant of No. 264 The Peak saw a real live tiger as he was returning from market early in the morning. The tiger was walking up Wanchai Gap, giving our 'boy' a good view of its stripes before it melted into the shrub like the feline magician that it was.

No doubt the majority of European expatriates in the 1920s also sincerely believed that they treated their amahs fairly. Amahs looked after the kids while the parents fulfilled their work and social obligations. But the masters and mistresses of the house needed to be vigilant about their local nannies because, while these women held a position of great responsibility in bringing up their European offspring, they sometimes had strange ideas. One such idea concerned Stripes.

For some children growing up in Hong Kong, especially Chinese children, the tiger was the bogeyman. Some amahs followed the tradition of teaching kids moral lessons with the aid of an avenging tiger that meted out justice. Seeing how many tiger reports were coming up, it seems a convenient device for keeping the kids on their toes. Western families had the equivalent in God almighty, in pious families, and some kind of supposed meritocratic work ethic in the more secular families. Many Western children growing up with the aid of a Chinese amah were also exposed to the Chinese traditions that perhaps the parents would not have approved of, or may not have known much about.

"Amahs have a good deal to recommend them; their wonderful patience and rather stolid temperaments are an excellent corrective to the excitable nerves of English children," wrote a columnist on a women's page in the *Hong Kong Telegraph* in 1927. The admiring correspondent was however concerned that amahs were scaring little Western kids too much with their beastly tales. The writer warns mothers to be watchful for horror stories told to a child, saying "irreparable damage may be done to its mental development."

Tigers and monkeys were said to be the favourite bogies of the amahs, and "no one who gave a moment's real thought would not be horrified at the idea of the pad, pad, of the fierce tiger who would come and devour a child because it had been naughty." The writer was greatly concerned about the psychological damage the tiger yarns did to the sensitive European mind, though presumably she was unconcerned about telling children lies about a bearded man that snuck down the chimney every Christmas.

The suggested remedy for the overly moralistic amah was to firmly tell her that she would be sacked if she did it again.

After such an unfortunate episode, the kids would need to be rehabilitated to regain their confidence. "Picture books which show animals in friendly postures can be illustrated by stories on *The Jungle*

Book lines giving an impression of the happy intimate life of the animals," the kindly writer explains. How the mother tiger is just like a human mother, teaching the kids to play and wash themselves and go on nice walks with them, all helps to restore that relaxed demeanour towards the wilderness.

The sacked amah meanwhile would be going back to a village, if she had one, where she could be reminded again just how nurturing a cattle-slaughtering big cat with slashing claws and razor-blade teeth could be.

The tiger that went to sea

Two years after the first Lee Garden tiger, a pair of hawkers brought a six-week-old cub to market on Hong Kong Island and offered it up to the Botanical Gardens at a price of $60, thinking perhaps the animal could be displayed for the public. But the government turned down the sellers saying it would be too expensive to build a suitable cage, and look after the big cat for the rest of its life. Lee Garden again featured in discussions, but nothing came of it and the cub ended up in the hands of Mr H. Green, superintendent of the Botanical and Forestry Department.

For a while Green kept the cub at his own residence. He hadn't advertised the fact, but the press caught wind of the yarn and came visiting to confirm the rumour. When the reporter got to the house he found Mrs Green hand-feeding it raw steak while it curled up in an improvised manger made from a Chinese wash basket filled with straw. At this point the carnivore just had four teeth, two in the top and two below.

After being with Green, the tiger next turned up in a surprising place, on the British warship HMS *Cumberland*, taking up a role as ship's mascot.

A visitor on the ship recounted that the human interest of the vessel was found on the quarterdeck where the mascot lived. "It is a most disarming, soft young thing with huge paws, and sharp, though as yet nicely behaved teeth, and an expression of innocence to counteract any of the natural fears attendant upon stroking its striped back."

This writer believed the tiger was lucky to be where it was. After being separated from its mother and a sibling, the cub had been at the mercy of hawkers seeking profit on Hong Kong Island. If it wasn't for good luck intervening in the nick of time "its fate eventually, as one reflects, would have been too horrible to conceive."

Commanding officer of the *Cumberland*, Capt. A.L. Snagge, said to be a man who was once "intimately associated" with Lawrence of Arabia, brought the six-week-old cub aboard. It wasn't the first exotic animal that Snagge had deployed on the ship, having earlier recruited an Abyssinian Oryx that the crew dubbed "Orace". There were critics of course who predicted that the hopelessly out-of-place feline would die in such a wrongful environment, but the impressed writer believed the nay-sayers had been proved wrong.

Returning to Hong Kong ten weeks after it first boarded the ship, the tiger was growing up to a healthy maturity. It was doted on by the crew and shown off to visiting dignitaries. They said it had a good character and never bared its teeth, unless some hapless greenhorn interrupted it while feeding.

The crew fed their mascot Marmite and "other sensible items," to keep it healthy and strong. And they said that Stripes had a good relationship with the ship's cat once the two felines got used to each other. They slept side-by-side, curling up together for their naps.

For some reason the doting sailors never quite settled on a name that stuck. The striped mascot was Clarence for a while, but then they decided that he didn't seem like a Clarence. For another brief period while still small and short-haired they called him Bonzo, like a shaven-headed Japanese monk, but that didn't stick either. After a while they settled into simply calling him "The Tiger".

From around 14 weeks the happy-go-lucky Stripes, who seemed to roam quite freely around the ship, gained a mysterious fascination for hatches. At 15 weeks he fell down the Captain's hatch, 'top to bottom,' in an incident that a diarist had noted was "inevitable." He survived that adventure well enough and sailed on to Shanghai.

The *Cumberland* patrolled the South China Sea and the China coast for the next decade, before heading to South American waters where it started its Second World War service against German raiders, and then to the African coast, followed by duties escorting Arctic convoys. The ship continued to serve after the war until 1958 when it was finally scrapped in England.

It would be interesting to think that a wild-caught Hong Kong tiger stayed on board throughout that time living out an illustrious career as a seafaring big cat. Alas, it was not to be. The hapless tiger, failing to learn from its earlier lesson, eventually, and perhaps inevitably, fell to its death down the Captain's hatch soon after its glowing Hong Kong report.

Man-eaters and the Blue Tiger
As some people in the colony followed the antics of a loveable little local cub that had been reduced to being a mascot, dozens of people were being eaten alive a few hundred miles to the north by wild beasts.

Man-eaters ravaged Fujian, where one district was being terrorised by a tiger gang that feasted exclusively on humans, and sought out travelling groups to select specific victims. Locals were paralysed with fear and not even the profit incentive from the heart, liver, skin and bones would induce them to confront the monsters in their mountains.

From the shelter that was Hong Kong, readers were consumed with horror as they came across stories of attacks that continued through the decade just outside of their own safe haven. Big cats that had grown so "venturesome" they would ambush in the daytime as well as at night. Ten people in a village either eaten alive or mauled within a week. One little girl who had a miraculous escape, knocked down by a tiger and seriously injured, but mercifully escaping death. The stories kept coming in.

The trouble was that emboldened predators were infesting well-populated areas where they would cause havoc. The beasts were caught sometimes when villagers organised and turned on their fanged tormentors with spikes, spears, crossbows and old guns. But the nightmare was just as often passed on when organising groups failed to finish the job, and instead drove wild animals onto neighbouring districts "where they continue their depredations."

Such tales of horror came from a land of mystery so inaccessible to the ordinary urbanites of Hong Kong that it might as well have been a far-off exotic foreign land, not the neighbouring province.

Early in the 1920s, a British gentleman representing the National Museum in Washington headed into "unknown China". Arthur de Carle Sowerby was on a quest to the heartland of the southern Chinese, where strange reports of beasts never imagined were insistently leaking to a curious outside world.

He travelled up the Min River to an old monastery in the mountains floating above the clouds 5,000 feet high in a wooded forest so rich in exotic vegetation that if a botanist dedicated three years to recording all the new flora, he said, there would still be work left over.

Sowerby met mountain people who looked more Malay or like aboriginal Formosans than like the Han Chinese that ruled the lower plains, whom the mountain locals looked on as an alien race of conquerors. These people spoke their own language, mixing Cantonese and Mandarin words into their strange tongue. It was a tough and wild environment and it was the heartland of the South China tiger.

Sowerby entered this dark and fabled land on a quest to find specimens of wonder and amazement. There were two species in particular that he was desperate to find, and for them he was willing to travel up savage river gorges and trek through endless jungle trails. He was willing to drown in torrential rains and burn dry on forbidding sun-scorched plains. These two species had never been caught alive and taken out of the ancient and crumbled Chinese empire.

One of them was a strange black and white cat-bear that has no tail, lives in the highlands on the Tibet border, eats only bamboo leaves, and was known as the panda. The pelt of the enigmatic panda had made it to the outside world, and a handful of very intrepid outsiders had seen the beast with their own eyes, but the creature had not made it out alive. Sowerby failed to achieve this dream, and no one else would do it either for more than another ten years, until a San Francisco socialite smuggled a cub onto a ship departing Shanghai in 1936.

His other target was the blue tiger.

This one he wanted dead or alive. No one then knew what a blue tiger was really like. It may be sky-blue, or periwinkle, or cobalt, or even Prussian blue, they said. It was very much wanted by zoologists. Sowerby was prepared "if necessary to hunt the beast to its lair in a cave, with the aid of torches, and shoot it at sight."

"The blue tiger is perhaps a distinct species," said Mr Sowerby, "and it is probably smaller than the Bengal tiger. Stories are told of it having been seen near the Chinese coast, but there is no specimen of it in any collection."

Unfortunately he never did capture a blue tiger dead or alive, though he did get a Chinese lizard named after him in later years, the *Lygosaurus sowerbyi*.

He must have been bitterly disappointed about the tiger because he was in the best possible company you could hope for if you were to hunt the blue tiger in China. He was in the company of Reverend Harry Caldwell, the original discoverer of the famous blue tiger.

Caldwell knew the South China tigers better than any other outsider: he lived among them, tracked them, killed them, watched them kill, feed, rest and rear their young. He comforted the relatives of their victims. He studied the predators in their lairs. He helped to distinguish the South China tiger as a distinctive subspecies.

He also saw blue tigers, though he never succeeded in getting one.

Chapter 6

GOD'S OWN TIGER SLAYER: THE STORY OF HARRY CALDWELL

The bible and the gun

"Late in the afternoon of a steaming summer's day in 1916 my wife and I were being rowed up the beautiful Min River in Fujian Province, south China. On the opposite shore a squalid village climbed from the water's edge into the smothering vegetation of the mountain side. As our half-naked boatmen swung the heavy junk across the river, gradually the massed humanity on the bank took shape. Blue-gowned men, tiny naked children, and women with silver knives flashing in their hair materialised from the drab background of mud and stone. Among them strode a tall man in a white pith helmet, moving restlessly up and down the steps and along the water's edge. We could see that he was built like a well-trained athlete; that he was nearly six feet tall and that a flashing smile seldom left his face in repose – intensely alive, bursting with enthusiasm, strenuously active! That was the quick impression of Harry R. Caldwell which registered on my mental retina even before I stepped out of the boat and grasped his hand."

– Roy Chapman Andrews,
American Museum of Natural History, 1924

I can't remember the part in the sermon on the mount where Jesus told his followers to love thy neighbour and go shoot some big cats. Yet for a certain brand of Christianity it is a given that true believers would carry a Bible in one hand and a gun in the other. One man who embraced that philosophy with enthusiasm was Harry Caldwell, American missionary and tiger hunter credited with dozens of kills over more than two decades. Though Caldwell was already a skilled hunter before arriving in the Far East with his beloved .22 high-power Savage rifle, he had never shot a tiger until he set foot in China in the early 1900s.

This man left what is probably the most vivid account in English of the South China tiger, an animal that is now functionally extinct. He got to know the big cat intimately well in its heartland, the same mysterious species that continued to visit Hong Kong regularly to the mid-1950s.

If we want to understand the Hong Kong tiger, we need to look at the stories that Harry Caldwell left behind.

Harry had a passion for God and his mission above all was to convert what he saw as the ignorant and superstitious people of the vast and ancient country to Christianity. At first on arrival in a land far, far away from his homeland, he saw no connection between his vocation and his shooting skills, and his gun was packed away for occasional holiday hunts. But when suffering from depression and loneliness in the isolated wild lands of the mission, he had a visit from a kindly bishop who advised him to pursue his hobbies to save himself from the abyss of doubt and despair. The moment Caldwell got his gun out was the moment he returned to the path of his own salvation, and in his view, it was the start of a process that brought hundreds of Chinese to Jesus.

Villagers of Fujian noticed that the American missionary was a keen hunter. They saw what he did with the wild boar, the muntjacs and the big-horned sheep up on the craggy tops. Tigers on the other hand were elusive and stealthy and at first Caldwell had no idea that God had sent him to the heartland of the South China tiger, the very lair of the beast. Not until the villagers told him so, once they had spotted his gun.

A man-eater started spreading terror and devastation in the Kutien hills one spring. The fear was like a crippling virus that spread through the mountain population. It was believed that the monster had eaten

250 people. It was sabre-toothed, they said, with supernatural powers. It could disappear at will.

Inside one cottage a baby played underneath a table where grown men sat smoking, telling tall tales and making predictions. From the blackness outside, the beast suddenly rushed in, smashing lanterns and throwing the table into the air, as it snatched the child in its massive jaws and thundered back into the night. The household was left in shock, horror and grief. Nearby, shepherds would disappear overnight, sometimes found later half-eaten and mangled. Crops were left untended.

The desperate villagers sent a magistrate to talk to the sharp-shooting missionary with the magic American rifle. Caldwell had seen that his hard work as a missionary was being undermined because people were too scared to leave their houses to attend the church that he had built. He made up his mind to accept the task and go to hunt the tiger, but, as he had never killed a tiger before, he needed to get some advice. He visited the British consul in Fuzhou who had previously been stationed in India, so was considered a likely experienced tiger hunter and font of tiger lore.

The pompous British official laughed at the wild American simpleton when he reported that a tiger was at large. "Tigers in Fukien?" he scoffed. "Only a missionary could dream up such a notion." Caldwell tried to elaborate with details from the land of nightmares over the hill, but the consul would have none of it.

"Reverend, I don't think you'd know the difference between a tiger and a civet cat if you met them both side-by-side," the grand old India hand concluded.

Considering the fact that the consul didn't even know there were tigers in the province he lived in, it is doubtful that he would have been able to give any advice useful in southern China. The British way of killing a tiger was to sit on top of an elephant and wait at a killing ground. Hundreds of Indian footmen would flush game out of the jungle by beating pots and clanging iron bars, as they closed in on a decreasing circle.

That method wouldn't have been practical in Fujian without elephants, and without a large body of native subjects who could be ordered or coerced as jungle-beaters. Lacking the support he had hoped to get from an assumed man of experience, Caldwell set out to lead the hunt for an animal he never encountered before, alongside his cook Dada.

He didn't know much about tigers at the time, but he knew about hunting other animals: shy, nimble and large beasts like deer and wild hogs. He knew about bears too and possibly wolves and mountain lions. Most of all he knew how to shoot his Savage. He reasoned that as a tiger was a big cat, and cats like to eat fish, there was a good chance that a tiger would also eat fish. He bought sardines from a market downtown and took them up to the tiger hills. To his frustration, no matter where he baited the big cat with fish, the Lord of the Hundred Beasts refused to reveal itself. No doubt the pompous consul would have enjoyed that.

Caldwell switched bait, from fish to goats. He placed the kids in a basket and hid them in the bush, bleating and pleading. The beast soon responded and Harry found himself face-to-face with a wild tiger for the first time in his life.

He took aim and missed.

It was unusual for him to miss and over the next few days he missed again as he came to realise there wasn't just one tiger, there were several. Suspecting his trusty Savage was out of line, he examined it and discovered the sight had been knocked. It turned out that villagers who had put him up in the tiger lands had admiringly passed the tiger-gun around each other one night as the big hunter slept. One of them had dropped the lethal weapon and inadvertently dislodged the sight. It was a seemingly insignificant incident that could have cut short Caldwell's tiger-shooting career and his life before he had even shot his first South China predator.

With the gun fixed, Caldwell was ready for the next encounter which came when he noticed the frantic twittering of birds. He threw a stone into the bushes where the sound was coming from.

He "couldn't have gotten no more violent reaction had he tossed a hand grenade. The whole slope exploded in one huge charging tiger," Harry's son John recounted years later.

Harry dropped his first tiger in one shot.

Caldwell strapped the carcass of the beast onto a river raft and headed downstream with his trophy. On the way to Fuzhou the launch got stuck on a sandbar for three hours and, exposed under the burning sun, the tiger swelled up into a huge bloated mound of dead meat. As soon as the procession hit the town, crowds swarmed in awe of the massive man-eating monster from the mountains. The pompous consul elbowed his way through the throng of sweaty, excited *hoi polloi* and stared at the wild animal that lay slain before him. He was so astounded that he completely dropped his arrogance and blurted, "I have lived in India and have seen many Bengal tigers, but never have I seen one as big or as beautiful as this."

The canny Caldwell hadn't quite forgotten the previous arrogance. "Is it a tiger?" he asked teasingly. And the befuddled nimrod fell hook, line and sinker. "Is it a tiger? Why man, it's the biggest tiger in creation!"

Caldwell, who must have been having a fantastic day, casually remarked that he had been thinking it might have been a civet cat. "Down country we have to chase them out of the backyard every morning." At which point I'm sure he would have high-fived Dada, his trusty cook, had this been happening a century later.

From then on Caldwell and Dada would become one of the greatest tiger hunting teams on record in China, with a total of 48 kills in Caldwell's name and Dada notching up 10 himself. Harry also became one of the most important authorities on the South China tiger, a breed that was at that time beginning to be recognised as a distinct subspecies. His son John later wrote that to all intents and purposes, Harry had discovered *panthera tigris amoyensis,* the South China tiger.

Caldwell would be sought out by experts from around the world wanting to get to know the South China variety. At the same time he noticed quickly that whenever he killed a tiger, more people would turn to Jesus, a fact that only fuelled his enthusiasm for killing tigers. When he was approached for a second time with a request to get a tiger, he responded eagerly. "I took with me both my Bible and my rifle, for I was bent upon a twofold mission in this long coveted field."

In tiger country

Having ruled out the British-Indian method of killing a tiger from the back of an elephant with the aid of an army of beaters, Caldwell considered the other options for pursuing his new-found vocation. One technique employed elsewhere was to sit in a tree and wait. But there was a problem in southern China: not enough suitable trees. Human migration to new lands had intensified in the 18th century and people had stripped the trees wherever they went in the never-ending quest for fuel.

Yet even with deforestation, sometimes Caldwell was amazed at the abundance of wildlife in the Fujian countryside. There was an occasion when he tied up a goat to wait for a tiger and was quickly rewarded by a stalking big cat. Things did not quite go to plan however when the careful creature spotted Caldwell and his partner. It crouched down in the grass and waited, flicking its tail tip intermittently, all senses on high alert. The tension levels rose even higher when a second tiger bounded into view, also attracted by the bleating goat. I doubt even Caldwell was happy with this situation, but the dynamic changed once again when a small number of deer came walking into the scene oblivious of the two massive striped carnivores hidden among the grasses. The tiger that had been so cautious all this time instinctively sprang to action nabbing a deer, and in doing so scattered the others in panic. One of them ran straight into the jaws of the second tiger and the pair of satisfied felines scuttled off to eat their prizes, having lost all interest in the bleating goat.

John, in his account of growing up a missionary son in pre-war China, also noted the abundance of wildlife even in the tree-depleted countryside. There were wild boars, wolves, foxes, a dozen species of pheasant, leopards and several other varieties of wild cat. There were deer of all sizes from rabbit-like muntjacs to the 600-pound sambar, and exotic mountain beasts like the giant goat-like serow with its donkey ears and flowing mane.

Yet every animal likes a free gift, and that is why Harry often used a tethered goat to lure the Lord. It seemed a sensible method – he got to choose the spot, arrange everything to his advantage and sit somewhere comfortable. Most people would stick to that, but Harry had a second trick up his sleeve, and that did not need the help of a goat. He would track a tiger to find its lair, wait until the tiger went off on the prowl, then put himself right inside of the lair and wait. He called that the "still" hunt and admitted that it was the most terrifying method, though he cheerfully noted that it gave him great opportunities to study the Lord of the Hundred Beasts in its own home.

Caldwell noticed that tigers would often favour certain places to eat their kills. These places were interesting to explore, giving insight to the range of food the 100 per cent carnivore would eat. He would find the skulls and bones of deer, boars, dogs, porcupines and even pangolins. When tigers eat mammals the surprisingly picky eaters start by using their big coarse tongue to scrape off the fur. Caldwell could spot the aftermath of a tiger meal easily by finding a circle of scattered fur. In the case of pangolins it would be the scales that were scraped off, which technically are made of clumped and hardened fur in any case. For local Chinese villagers pangolin scales were a source of wealth, a well-known and powerful medicinal ingredient. Intrepid collectors would risk life and limb to raid these dangerous tiger feasting terraces in the pursuit of health and wealth.

Really the tigers ate anything, and sometimes had unexpected preferences. A frog hunter became the victim of a tiger attack one evening as he walked home with a haul of frogs. The tiger stalked the helpless man, pounced on him and killed him. His body was left otherwise intact, but the net that held the frogs was ripped to shreds and every single frog had been consumed.

The tiger is a pussy cat

Caldwell would spend days at a time in tiger-infested ravines, watching and getting to know them intimately. He learned that the beasts were complex characters. On one hunt he led a goat into a ravine that he recognised to be the lair of a tiger. He tied up the sacrifice and hid himself in a safe spot, holding his gun as the poor kid bleated for its life. A tiger quickly arrived, lured in by the sound. It came close enough for Caldwell to observe, but not close enough for a clear shot. He watched it for more than an hour and he sensed that the King of the Forest was quite correctly suspicious. In his eyes, Caldwell saw the tiger as a monster-sized tabby cat, nervously putting a paw forward as if to pounce, then retracting a moment later, overcome with hesitation.

When the master predator did finally make a decisive move, it flattened itself so close to the ground that to Caldwell it moved "like a striped serpent." Its chin and throat touched the ground, and every muscle strained. It swiftly slid forward with apparently no other movement than the "quivering of the shoulders and hips." Then the beast made three flying leaps onto the terrace where the goat was tethered and stopped dead to stare at Caldwell, clearly visible 25 feet away.

"At this point it became necessary for me to fire the shot that finished this wonderful study," Harry concluded.

For all the reputation of terrifying fierceness, Caldwell discovered that the species was extremely cautious, to the point of timidity sometimes. On one occasion, the patient Caldwell observed a tiger looking for three hours at a captive goat until it made its move. Another hunt brought a tiger within 30 feet of live bait, only for the skittish cat to scarper when it noticed that there were grass cutters 500 yards away.

Perhaps the issue was about control. There is no shortage of stories about outrageously audacious tiger attacks. Caldwell recalls that the very same tiger that was intimidated by grass cutters 500 yards away slaughtered a cow just 10 yards from its owner, who was squatting on a dyke eating his lunch with his back to the cow. The predator doesn't like to be surprised, but it is willing to take risks when it believes its stalking has been perfected to the point of invisibility, until the final explosive charge.

Don't mess with the tiger

Another thing that Caldwell noticed was that the supreme predator of the hills did not always appear to attack out of need. Like humans, tigers appear to have a temper. He recalled a deer hunter in a forest who made the stupendous mistake of disturbing a sleeping tiger. The furious beast leapt up, clamped its jaws shut on the foot of the annoying primate and dragged him through the forest. The desperate man clung to a small tree, and though the tiger could have easily finished him off, it appeared satisfied with the lesson it had meted out and walked away from the broken man, leaving him writhing in agony.

Another tiger reacted with a more deadly rage when it was disturbed by three fuel hunters. It crushed the skull of one, snapped the neck of the other, and killed the third outright with a mighty swipe of its paw that flung the victim down to a terrace below. The moody monster walked off without making any attempt to eat its victims.

Another case suggests that the tiger is as capable of lashing out in misdirected anger as we are. It started with the tiger on the attack, grabbing a village boy by sinking its fangs into his skull and carrying him off. The father went ballistic and chased the beast with every drop of strength he had in him. Even a tiger is slowed down when it is carrying a boy, so the man was able to keep up with the beast, harassing it with all his might. Eventually the exasperated feline dropped its prize and walked off, killing the first human it came across without making any effort to carry him off for food.

Caldwell also saw that tigers could be just as needlessly lethal even without an outrage that triggers it. He shot one that killed a live lure he had placed and was surprised to open up its stomach and see it full of freshly eaten dog. The predator had apparently killed for the sake of it. Perhaps such an observation comes as no surprise to any cat owner who has seen their pet kill and discard a carcass without showing any sign of being driven by hunger. The resemblance does not end there. It becomes more chilling.

In 1914, on the trail of a man-eater, locals found the scattered remains of a teenage boy in a tiger's lair. It was a horrifying and deeply sad discovery. The fact that no teenager had been reported missing in the nearby villages may have been of some consolation to the people of the district, but it raised the possibility that the lad had been dragged from a distance. According to Caldwell the evidence pointed to the likelihood the boy was alive on reaching the lair. The place was smeared with fresh blood, suggesting the predator had kept him alive and tortured him, "just as a cat tortures and plays with a mouse so long as there is life in it."

Dogs buckle at the sight of a tiger

Sometimes tigers perform feats of strength that are difficult to fathom. One place Caldwell came across had been the site of an extraordinary cow theft from what should have been a secure pen. The farmer must have been confident when he carved a pen out of the hillside rock face that his cottage backed onto. The only entrance to the pen was through the cottage; the other sides were embedded in the mountain. Yet a tiger dropped down into the pit, grabbed the cow and leapt 12 foot with it in its mouth, and carried it off over the hill. Villagers explained to Caldwell that tigers would carry their kills by hauling them onto their backs.

Yet this apparently bionic beast did have a weakness. Harry learned from the locals that if a tiger charged, you should bolt downhill. It was well known by villagers that the big cat is slow and clumsy down a hill because its front legs are shorter than its back legs. It was a piece of wisdom that rippled through the folklore network of southern China and was taught to children in Hong Kong.

At one point Caldwell considered importing American bear hounds to help in the war against tigers. He thought it was theoretically possible to use them effectively, but only after tigers had been taught to fear them.

The problem was that the local power balance for tigers and dogs was completely weighted in favour of tigers. The dogs of southern China were terrified of the tiger, for the obvious reason that tigers regularly ate them up. Caldwell heard an unfortunate dog tale when a tiger attacked a cow that was being watched over by a couple of young shepherds. The boys were on a rock and their dog was sleeping below them when the sneak attack burst out of nowhere. Instinctively the boys yelled and screamed, raising a racket that snapped the dog out of its slumber.

The canine leapt into the air and shot straight to the scene of horror. The cow was struggling and writhing, unable to get up from the ground with its neck broken. The tiger had backed off a little and was watching from the shade, waiting for its dinner to die. The dog, so full of bravado until that moment, spotted the Lord of the Hundred Beasts lurking in the bush, spun 180 degrees in the air and bolted. It didn't get far, as it suffered a massive heart attack and dropped dead.

It was obvious that the South China tiger would not be afraid of American bear hounds when they first met them. Those hounds bred for attack wouldn't be afraid of the tiger either. They would throw themselves at the target and there would be an inevitably high attrition rate as the tiger would swat them one after another. Caldwell considered that the tigers would eventually learn to fear the dumb unrelenting viciousness of the pack, and presumably would then become more easily intimidated and therefore controllable. But he decided that the cost in dog lives would be too high and it wouldn't be a practical method in southern China.

Summer time, and the living's uneasy

Escaping their residence in the heart of tiger country one summer, Harry took his wife and kids up a cool and breezy mountain, for the traditional seasonal retreat from the heat of the plains, and installed his household at an isolated mountain monastery surrounded by ferocious man-eating tigers.

Other than the sheer beauty of the place and its ideal setting, the presence of big cat predators was the main reason Caldwell chose to spend summer there. The local feline predators were known to be capable of rushing through an open door and dragging a fully-grown adult out of his house. Harry's holiday activity would be to kill man-eaters.

He was well aware of the dangers before he brought his family to their summer retreat. When he visited the spot to check it for suitability, he of course had his high-powered Savage with him. After securing the deal with the friendly mountain monks, he took a hike up the hillsides and nabbed an opportunistic hunt, tumbling a magnificent tiger off a rock.

"He proved to bear all the ear-marks of a real old man-eater," he wrote, now well on his way to expert status in the field. He returned to the monastery triumphant, pleased to have been of some use, and pleased to be able to carry out God's work.

The monks were not that impressed. They told him that there were plenty more in the lair, all of them man-eaters, just like this one.

"Plans for taking my wife and children to such a place began to be attended with considerable misgivings," he admitted, "but I determined to go through with the adventure."

It is difficult to understand how Mrs Caldwell agreed to this madcap venture, but there she was on holiday with the kids. They had left their home in tiger country to vacation in the tigers' lair. Reckless Harry went out shooting off his gun as she and the kids amused themselves in the relatively safe environment of the monastery grounds.

Unfortunately Harry wasn't having much luck at the beginning of his holiday. He followed a goat-thieving cat to a natural bowl where he called in a group of volunteers to flush it out. He analysed the shape of the landscape and the line of trails to predict where the beast would reappear. He saw it emerge, stand for a second and swing around behind a pine tree.

"Then he began to stalk me," Caldwell grimly reported.

It poised with ears flat against its head and crouched for an attacking leap.

"Just recall how your kitten used to look when about to spring upon a spool attached to the end of a string and you can appreciate what this animal looked like."

Caldwell fired, but missed, splintering the trunk of a pine tree. It was a frustrating failure, but did enough to reverse a situation where the odds were stacked up against him, by spooking the stalking predator away.

The next day Harry pushed on through after a tiger that had just killed a boy. Once again he got himself into an encounter that was a huge risk to his own state of health, but was also an opportunity to score a fatal shot.

Once again he missed.

In a case where history was repeating itself, Caldwell unearthed an incident that was beginning to look like an occupational hazard. As happened previously, his hosts, this time the monks, had taken great fancy to the tiger-gun and had been inspecting it in detail as he slept, and once again a careless dimwit had knocked the sight out of line. How did Caldwell, the famed hunter, keep allowing this to happen? It makes you wonder if back in the 1920s people were more carefree, or just a bit mad.

Then came the day when he really should have listened to his wife.

Harry's son John recalls that his mother looked out of the monastery window and saw three tigers. Harry was sceptical – tigers are not social, they don't normally hang about in groups. But he went out to investigate, to humour his wife according to John. He went with just six shells, and ten minutes later he was face to face with five tigers.

Interestingly enough, Harry's own account is different. He said he responded to village reports of a tiger that caused havoc among children and farm animals. He had somehow been separated from his load carrier, and was left with only six cartridges when he came face to face with five tigers, he recalled with no mention of his wife's observation.

From this point, father and son's two accounts tell more or less the same story. They are in agreement that Harry only had six cartridges. He followed a trail and came across five tigers. One spotted him immediately and crouched down for an attack. The crack-shot missionary let a bullet fly that hit the tiger and spun it in the air. He failed to kill it, and the injured beast scarpered uphill. Five bullets to go and he shot through

*He went with just six shells, and ten minutes
later he was face to face with five tigers*

four of them going after the wounded cat that finally fell with a blood-curdling howl. He was left with one bullet and four tigers on the loose. He used that last one with a clean shot that eliminated his last kill of the day.

"Now I found myself in the awkward position of having an empty gun in hand and having three tigers stalking around me," he wrote with the beautifully stylish understatement of a bygone era.

He only had one option, to sit very still. And that is how he survived the three man-eaters surrounding him.

When he felt sure they had gone, he came down the mountain with two carcasses and was greeted by an emotional crowd. Villagers seethed with anger for the suffering the venerable Lords of the Hills had meted out on them. One man tried to beat a carcass with his hoe, while an elderly lady screamed and thumped the other for carrying away her only child and breaking up her home.

The power of human magic

The villagers were not always paralysed by fear.

Caldwell went after one big cat into its lair one day, only to miss and splinter the wood of a pine tree. The local clairvoyant looked into the matter and on account of the tiger being so daring, declared it a "big ruler god." In doing so, the mystic promised the villagers success on a hunt as long as they promised to bring back the pelt as an offering. This ruling was enough to set off a hundred locals armed with pikes, poles, crossbows and old guns loaded with rusty nails and slugs. They found the "god" and laid into it with their brickbats and makeshift weapons. But the tiger kept charging back at the braves and the situation looked precarious.

The tide turned when a man arrived on the scene with an old European double-barrelled shotgun. He fired two shots and one of them hit but didn't stop the ferocious beast from charging. The shooter dropped to the floor and flattened himself down in the grass.

It was enough to throw off the seething feline which randomly diverted its attention to the nearest man, who dived straight into an irrigation pool. The furious cat then turned and flung itself towards a fellow on the terrace below, missed him, and landed in a potato field. It desperately wanted a victim. Punishment must be delivered. So it drew deeply on all its remaining life-force, gathered itself for the next thundering charge, and dropped dead.

The villagers had stood the beast down and won. Changing the minds of people once almost paralysed by fear to being ready to confront a huge and vicious wild animal with nothing but sharpened poles and rusty muskets takes one hell of a placebo. The spells of a village shaman can inspire and bring results so dramatic that perhaps it is justified to call it magic.

However, there was one magic that the American hunter-missionary believed in more completely than he could the shaman's placebo. Perhaps he knew it was even more instrumental than the God of the New Testament. It was the bullet. His own description of a bullet's effect is so vivid that it makes you wonder how he possibly thought shooting tigers really was Christian work.

"The big cat lunged into the air, coming down dead," he wrote. "The ball entered the stomach cavity, doing terrible execution. Had the animal swallowed an explosive bomb the results could not have been more disastrous. No animal could sustain such a shock and live to do much damage."

Amen.

Blue tiger up close

Caldwell had a clear fascination for nature, and a passion for studying the ecology around him. He became renowned, not only for his reputation for shooting tigers dead, but also for his knowledge of bird life, reptiles, other mammals and the vast array of plants of Fujian and the Min valley. He became a contributor of biological notes on southern China birds to Geoffrey Herklots' university biological journal *Hong Kong Naturalist*. Experts such as Roy Chapman Andrews of the American Museum of

Natural History made epic trips to the heart of China's darkness to spend time, usually hunting, with the legend that was Caldwell.

With a good track record for his observations, and the weight of his self-earned scientific credibility propping up his reputation, Caldwell curiously became obsessed with a tiger that he believed was a new species. He was so affected by it that he named his best-selling book after this curiosity, the blue tiger.

The behaviour of this anomaly doesn't sound much different from other tigers Caldwell described himself, but there was a belief that it was more fierce, more devastating and deadly than the 'normal' yellow and black tigers. It rushed into a house to grab a child that was playing under a table while men sat around smoking. We heard the same story from Caldwell earlier, except it was a normal stripey monster that succeeded in carrying off a toddler. In this account the blue missed its target, clamping its jaws on the table leg, and bolted off with it.

The locals called it the Black Devil and inevitably said that it had magic powers. They said that of stripey tigers too. Caldwell saw it, and noted that it had a blue sheen to it rather than black. Perhaps it was like a blue whistling thrush which looks black in the shade but is a deep velvet blue in the sunlight. He called it a Maltese blue.

Today's tiger literature acknowledges rare melanism in tigers, the same phenomenon that produces black panthers. A melanistic animal is naturally the same species as its normal-coloured parents, but it has a condition in its pigments that causes it to be dark. Caldwell noted that the stripes were clearly visible over the blue. Tasmanian tiger snakes are also a suitably awesome black with black stripes, just a difference in tone that is visible in certain angles of light.

Caldwell got close to shooting the blue that he so desperately wanted. One came close to his hide and his finger was on the trigger. The big blue cat was cautiously moving towards the usual goat sacrifice, but it was distracted by movement in the valley below. Caldwell realised that there were two boys cutting grass and that they were in danger. He feared that a shot could injure the tiger and tumble it into the valley. There would be no telling what an enraged and injured tiger might do to two boys in its path. Instead of pulling the trigger Harry stood up shouting, causing the tiger to crouch down in the long grass in silence to assess the strange situation. That was long enough to let the boys head out of danger, but when Caldwell made his move to stalk, the blue tiger had disappeared.

Caldwell's enthusiasm for the blue tiger was so great and infectious that Andrews of the American museum, who had his own reputation as a famed zoologist, adventurer, collector and raconteur, made a special trip to Fujian to specifically look for the rare prize, a possible new species of tiger.

Unfortunately the dream team never succeeded.

If Harry Caldwell saw a blue tiger, it is likely that there really was a tiger that was blue-looking. When you read his no-nonsense descriptions of the Chinese wilderness everything he says rings true, and most of it can be corroborated. He describes with vivid and unsentimental clarity. He was already so full of wonder about the nature he saw, and shot, that there wouldn't have been any special need to make stuff up. And though there are no scientific records of a blue in captivity, or a skin, many scientists are satisfied that melanism is theoretically possible in a wild tiger. What Caldwell was wrong about was that he was looking at a different species of tiger.

He might also have been wrong that the behaviour of the blue was different from normal tigers. He believed that the blue was more ferocious. There is no doubt that the destruction he attributed to the blue was devastating enough – whole families slaughtered, discovery of the bones of a missing 11-year-old girl, scores of people dead, to name some of his examples. But by Caldwell's own accounts, the blue's achievements in evildoing do not stand out from other man-eaters he described. There were many horrors.

How to really shoot a tiger

This is one of the sobering facts about the Lord of the Hundred Beasts. The species is beautiful and genuinely awesome, and yet capable of merciless death and destruction. The Chinese called it venerable. You cannot help but admire it, but you know it is dreadful. It can be a horror, a nightmare, and a cruel and savage serial-killer. This is no anthropomorphic judgement of character. It is the simple lived experience of millions of people who have coexisted with man-eating tigers.

Despite the terrible reputation it is interesting that unarmed humans have succeeded in intimidating tigers through bravado and illusion. When Caldwell was caught out without a gun by a charging tiger on a hillside, he repeatedly opened and shut an umbrella in the direction of the beast. That was enough to put the big cat off, causing it to slink away confused.

In Hong Kong, as elsewhere in China, villagers afraid of tigers after dark walked around banging gongs. They were helpless, but there was an understanding that they could still intimidate a massive predator. When tigers were around in the hills all over southern China, flimsily armed boys and girls stayed close to their cattle to protect their assets.

And that could be what characterises the general power balance between people and tigers – humans hold the tiger at bay, when they do, by subduing its spirit. Yet one slip, one unguarded child, one sneaky attack from behind, and the edifice of deceit collapses. We have also seen this in certain breeds of domesticated dogs.

Perhaps folklore and local knowledge can hold that tiger off for years on end when the right factors in the environment somehow remain balanced. But Caldwell's accounts vividly illustrate that the power balance often fell apart and disaster could hit communities. Ultimately such events were the South China tiger's undoing in a heavily populated and rapidly changing habitat. The tigers became too bold, too visible and too deadly. The traditional shamanism of human bravado crumbled in a catastrophic collapse of confidence. The new leaders of a modern weaponised world would soon decide that living with the predator was no longer an acceptable risk.

A difficult question is how much the actions of the well-meaning God-fearing hunter-missionary helped to bring about the demise of the species. Caldwell achieved what he set out to in the early years of his tiger mission; he helped to dispel the myth of the invincible tiger. In a strange parallel, just as humans can hold tigers at bay with tricks, bluff and death-defying confidence, so the tiger can spin its own spells of invincibility and sacred undefeatable wrath. When Caldwell found his parishioners crippled by the evil magic of the dreadful tiger god, he saw superstition, ignorance and fallen souls.

He proved many times over that one or two calm, focussed people equipped with the right tools could stop a divine and vengeful man-eater in its tracks. His own cook, Dada, earned a reputation as Harry's right-hand man, and a tiger hunter in his own right. In a gesture that was as practical as it was symbolic, Dada cut his traditional queue hair plait off after he became precariously trapped in thorns on a tricky tiger hunt with Harry. After that he went on to bag ten tigers in his own name, and proved that being Chinese was no hindrance to going after otherworldly superpowers. That was a lesson that proved essential to the anti-tiger brigades of the 1950s that finished the South China tiger off.

To Harry, his hunting achievements were integral to his mission work, and another spin-off from it is that he became a trusted negotiator who helped to mediate between often corrupt government officials and violent warlords who had been driven to a life of banditry. Ultimately he saw himself as a man on a peace mission, and no doubt there would have been many willing to testify that the actions of this brave man helped to save lives, perhaps hundreds of lives.

We don't know if Caldwell had any notion of how precarious the tiger population would become in the second half of the 20th century, but at some point he converted from faith in his much loved Savage to an allegiance to the camera. He used the techniques he had developed as a hunter to stalk a big cat, stake out its lair and sit and wait. As soon as a big cat appeared he would shoot it, with film. Unfortunately much of the footage he had collected was lost in the chaotic Japanese invasion and left behind when the Caldwells eventually left China in 1944.

Harry Caldwell lived the rest of his life in Nashville, Tennessee, and died in 2006 at the age of 94. Imagine the stories he had for his grandchildren.

Chapter 7

MYSTERY CATS, BLACK TIGERS AND MAN-EATERS

1930 – 1940

Suspicious cats

The 1930s start with another sceptical description from a local Chinese source. An "inhabitant" of the New Territories "claims" to have seen the tiger, a specific tiger that was known about. A woman had seen it kill a cow a month earlier near Tai Po. Now this beast had turned up on the small island of Tsing Yi where it killed a pig and carried it off. There were lots of scare quotes, making clear that the editor was no fool, and he treated the colourful anecdotes with all the weary doubt required. Yet as the decade rolled on, the scare quotes would become redundant as tiger sightings piled in, one after another, until educated people in the colony more-or-less came to accept that they lived in a land where the Lord of the Hundred Beasts was a regular visitor. But that would take time.

When the driver of motor car 629 on Castle Peak Road saw a tiger crossing the brick works at Tsuen Wan in the spring of 1931 around the same time a Chinese person spotted "Mister Stripes" at Castle Peak police station, someone important at the *Hong Kong Sunday Telegraph* evidently felt it necessary to point out that "taken either separately or collectively, no great credence might be placed on these reports."

What a strange, stubborn and tediously dull comment to make in the face of a wild tiger on your beat, on your watch. Why wouldn't a series of reports, constantly and consistently drip-feeding the readership year after year, not be taken collectively to give credence to the fact that big cats roamed in and out of Hong Kong every year? In the context of the collected accounts throughout the 1920s, and what we now know would continue to emerge into the 1950s, the reports of March 1931 seem perfectly plausible. Yet without looking backwards, or being able to look forwards, editors constantly betrayed their incredulity and ultimately their ignorance about the environment they lived in.

The farmer at the centre of the story said one of his pigs had been killed by some animal "the nature of which is unknown." The predator was a mystery: a mystery cat perhaps? An animal that could kill a pig. He was advised to take the carcass to the police station where they could make a proper examination. Somehow, even if tiger visits in Hong Kong were treated as fantasy, the police had enough experience to be able to examine a carcass and divine the nature of the beast that killed it.

The police did have the experience – at least those in the New Territories did. An earlier sighting was recalled, one in which terror-stricken Chung Fat-tai, a villager at Fung Yuen in Tai Po, watched her cow gored by Stripes. She screamed so hideously the predator gave up on its kill, bounded back into the hillside and melted into the bush. Sergeant Tuckett of Tai Po police investigated the crime scene and found six-and-a-half-inch, five-clawed paw marks on the shoulders of the victim. But let's not forget "taken either separately or collectively, no great credence might be placed."

Perhaps it is understandable that people in Hong Kong were suspicious of tiger tales. After all, despite the evidence that they did appear, their trail of destruction was not very significant compared to what happened in other parts of China, and in other colonial territories such as Malaya and India. It almost feels that, so revered as the regal feline is, real tiger stories could only belong in more exotic places. In India's Bihar and Orissa, there was a report that 70 people had been killed by man-eaters in the first eight months of 1932. In Patna a few years earlier, there was a spate of man-eating until a huge beast was finally dropped by a police

She screamed so hideously the predator gave up on its kill,
bounded back into the hillside and melted into the bush

superintendent. They opened it up to find a human foot lodged in its guts.

Hong Kong's big cat stories could not compete with tales of such horror and wonder. They were of the fleeting appearances of vagrants. It seems that bringing undue attention to themselves by transgressing local rules was the last thing the feline scavengers wanted. They stuck to low-level crime, focussed on livestock, kept themselves shadowy and inconspicuous and wove a cloak of mystery. They used tiger sorcery to melt into the bush any time the humans were out looking for them.

Wolves were reported, as were other wild dogs. Of course such animals can kill domestic pigs and possibly cattle, though they would only do that in packs. Feral dogs still kill wild boar piglets occasionally. There were always alternative explanations for slaughtered livestock in the territory. One report said pigs had been stabbed to death around the time a tiger was seen. Why would anyone stab pigs to death? Perhaps teenage boys of every generation have done strange things to animals, but what is most likely to explain the killing of a large domestic animal when there were tigers in the vicinity?

The simpler approach would be to accept the tiger as the most likely explanation and the stabbings as a fallback if for some reason the tiger was ruled out, not the other way round. That works if you accept the idea that tigers were regular visitors. It would seem that a person perhaps most qualified to make that call, who was tasked with setting up the biology faculty of the leading academic institution of the land, and working also as a top civil servant looking after the colony's forestry, had no problem accepting the fact that the South China tiger was a regular visitor.

Hong Kong's biologist

Geoffrey Herklots joined Hong Kong University in 1928 to start up the biology department, according to Malcolm Peaker who was a faculty member in later years. In 1937 Herklots took up a government post, alongside his university duties, as Superintendent of the Botanical and Forestry Department. He founded, edited and prolifically contributed to the *Hong Kong Naturalist* journal which has left a fantastic record of the territory's wildlife between 1930 and the arrival of the Japanese in 1941. His report on the 1929 Tai Po tiger is much more detailed than what was in the general press, and it had none of their worldly-wise nod-and-a-wink scepticism either.

He wrote:

"On the afternoon of 29th December a Chinese village woman was driving a cow to the village of Fung Yuen at the eastern side of Tolo Harbour opposite Tai Po. Near a ravine bordered by thick scrub-wood about a mile from the village a tiger sprang out from the thicket onto the back of the cow, biting and mauling the animal severely. The woman's screams frightened the animal which made off up the hillside. The cow struggled onward for about 100 yards, then lay down and ultimately died. Sergt. Tuckett visited the spot and examined the victim which showed unmistakable signs of having been mauled by a tiger."

Later on someone by the name of Mr E.I. Wynne Jones came to the site where the uneaten dead cow lay. He brought with him a goat and two chow dogs which he tied up to tempt the tiger with additional incentive, and set himself up with his hunting rifle in a strategic spot. He waited four hours and went home empty-handed as the tiger didn't make another appearance. Herklots notes that the tiger was spotted at another village two miles away that afternoon, and then a few days later a tigress with two cubs was seen near Tai Po Market.

In a speech Herklots gave on Hong Kong's wildlife to the Rotary Club in 1932, he stated matter-of-factly: "Tigers visit the Colony almost every year." He said they came from the wild country at the back of Bias Bay (today's Daya Bay). "Two were on Tai Mo Shan for several days during the spring of this year." He also mentioned that leopards would occasionally visit, and one was trapped and shot the year before.

The leopard was caught at Chung Pui, north of the Pat Sin Leng range in an area where villagers used illegal deer traps. A woman was cutting grass when she heard a noise she assumed to be a trapped deer. She called down to villagers to let them know and a man came up expectantly. When he got to the spot where the trap had been laid he couldn't find it, only seeing the broken rope that had tied it to a tree. Suddenly he was attacked by a wild cat with a deer trap clamped on its foot. The ferocious animal badly mauled the man's face and head, though he refused to go to hospital, a fact that gives us another clue that the number of reported big cat events in Hong Kong is almost certainly the minimum that occurred.

Though still vicious, the injured animal wasn't able to move far. It was helpless while armed men were fetched to finish it off. The beast was skinned and its flesh, bones, skull, teeth, whiskers and claws were auctioned off raising $150. The skin ended up at Sha Tau Kok police station where, with the permission of Sergeant Coleman, Herklots photographed it and published the image in *Hong Kong Naturalist*.

Years later, after internment under the Japanese at Stanley prison camp, Herklots published in 1951 a collection of his wildlife jottings in a book called *The Hong Kong Countryside*. The following is what he had to say then about the Lord of the Hundred Beasts:

"Nearly every winter one or more tigers visit the New Territories; often the visitor is a tigress with or without cubs. The visit rarely lasts more than two or three days. A tiger thinks nothing of a 40 mile walk and in a couple of nights could walk from the wild country behind Bias Bay to Tai Mo Shan or the Kowloon hills. Because their visits are usually of such short duration and because most people exaggerate, little credence is given to tiger rumours. Most that I have investigated have been founded on fact."

These are the words of the founder of Hong Kong University's biology department, and the territory's most authoritative biologist of his time. He made a clear, simple statement of fact that tiger visits happened. He made the point in 1932 in a public lecture, and repeated it in his 1951 book. His deduction was based on documented evidence.

In *The Hong Kong Countryside* he noted that a tigress with two cubs had been seen at Pan Chung, near Tai Po Market, in January 1931. He recorded several sightings and signs in 1934 including pig carcasses that showed the killer's fangs and eye-witness accounts from bird-hunters and woodsmen. He described a deer that ran for its life after an encounter and got stuck in a marshy pig-weed pond in a village. The tiger dared not enter the human village, but roamed about outside, trampling on vegetable plots and indenting the soil with its massive footprints.

Herklots believed that the same big cat was seen again. An old woman grass-cutter found herself under serious threat when the beast appeared, approached and started circling her. The terrified lady summoned up every drop of courage she had and whacked the feline repeatedly with her grass-carrying pole. This did the trick. Two hundred pounds of muscle power, predatory adrenaline, razor-blade claws and stabbing fangs set in high-pressure clamping jaws turned meekly, undoubtedly bewildered, and crept away from an alarming old lady with a pole.

The biologist often bemoaned the difficulty of convincing people that tigers really did visit Hong Kong. He sent two assistants to investigate a sighting over at Kowloon Reservoir equipped with plaster-of-Paris to take impressions of the paw-prints. "They returned with three or four excellent casts but even then many doubted the tale," he wrote.

A decade later, after the war, when the Bishop of Hong Kong sent Herklots a message that a large cat, "probably a tiger" walked across his lawn at Shatin, and enclosed his sketches of pug marks, again the biologist had no difficulty in accepting the proposition. He had the background knowledge to know it was perfectly plausible, and yet, "many were sceptical even of a bishop's evidence."

Dog seen carrying pig snout

A pig's foot was found under a bush outside a village near Tsuen Wan. The pig, to which the foot had been attached, had been carried off from the village the previous night, R.A. Pereira tells us in Herklots' *Hong Kong Naturalist*. When Pereira was told by a villager in November 1934 that a tiger had taken the pig, and eaten all of it under the bush except that foot, he was initially sceptical and thought wolves were the more likely culprits.

More pig reports followed two weeks later. Three killed, one taken away. A policeman at Tsuen Wan saw carcasses with clear signs of the killer's fangs.

Another couple of weeks later, a large pig disappeared at night near Tsung-lung, and in the morning a village dog was seen carrying a pig snout. The dog on its own would not have been able to kill and consume the big fat pig that had disappeared.

Towards the end of December Pereira set out with a pair of cousins to shoot some birds on the hills. They left the village of Tai Wo and climbed up to a place called Tang-Um where they heard a distant roar. It made them nervous, but they decided it was probably some bamboo horn blown by a villager. Then another roar came and a woodcutter appeared and helpfully pointed out a tiger about 400 to 500 yards away. All four of them got a clear view of the "magnificent animal" walking into the woods on the hillside. They were around three miles from a place called Lo Wai, Tsuen Wan. They only had a light shotgun, which would not have been effective on a predator of such magnitude and splendour.

On New Year's Eve someone saw the beast near Pak Siak Kiew, chasing a deer. The panicked ungulate bounded straight through a village. The tiger avoided the main street, but ran through a narrow alley and ended up jumping into an enclosed vegetable patch where it trampled all over the carefully cultivated plants before jumping back out the way it came in. Pereira measured the 7.5-inch spoors himself. He joined the group scouring the hills for half a day and sat up all night in waiting, but the mystery cat disappeared.

Although all trace of the animal was lost, Pereira was convinced it would return. This once-tiger-sceptic no longer needed convincing. Thanks to the editorship of Hong Kong's top biologist, we still have this record of a tiger visit in a biological journal, written up without the vagaries, innuendo and speculation of the general press. It fit into the overall view held by Herklots that *panthera tigris amoyensis* was indeed the top predator of the territory, other than man.

The tiger is not the only lost species that Herklots documented. Though he was better known as a botanist, he collected accounts of all lifeforms in Hong Kong. Thanks to him we know of the large musk shrews that used to enter houses in the New Territories, making a chattering noise like jangling coins and emitting an offensive stink. He kept records of native macaques that inhabited all the islands before today's feral monkeys came to rule over Kowloon. There were red dogs or dholes spotted in packs of four from the Kai Tak aerodrome to Castle Peak. Otters had been seen on Hong Kong Island, not just out at Lantau and over at Mai Po. Today just two civet cat species are known to inhabit the woods, the Indian and the masked palm civets. Herklots recorded a third, the Chinese civet, the largest of the family. It was a rare nocturnal omnivore, with a fondness for papaya and known as the "commanding officer" in local lingo for its three rank-giving stripes on its neck.

The pangolin still survives in Hong Kong, according to Kadoorie Farm, an NGO that started in the 1950s to aid local farmers and operates today as a conservation and educational centre. The presence of pangolins is a fact that is almost miraculous considering the species is the most trafficked mammal on the planet and has been driven to extinction in most of its range throughout Asia. It was already a protected species in the 1930s when Herklots was writing about it. He noted its toothless tube-like mouth and tongue that extends a "considerable distance" to slurp up termites, ant larvae, bees and wasps. He also noted then that the animal was persecuted for its strange scales that some believed had mystical medical properties. Thousands of skins used to be imported from Java to China before the trade was outlawed. I wonder if he would be surprised to learn that this defenceless little beast outlasted the tiger in southern China.

Another remarkable animal that appeared during Herklots' time in Hong Kong was the dugong. They were a real rarity even then. In fact it is unlikely that Herklots would have expected to hear of one at all. There were practically no records of the chubby odd-faced marine mammal in Chinese waters, and the biologist had to go back to a 1665 document to find any reference to the animal near the Pearl River delta. "It is therefore of particular interest to record that a dugong was caught near Hong Kong in 1940 or 1941 and brought into the city where it was photographed, skinned and I believe stuffed."

Sadly, other than the published accounts in the archives of *Hong Kong Naturalist*, the biologist's own field notes, along with so much documentation at Hong Kong University, were destroyed in the firestorm that was the Japanese invasion and occupation. During that period our resident expert was interned at Stanley prison camp where he was closely involved in welfare and education, according to Peaker. He was a member of the Camp Temporary Committee and gave lectures on biology, while working to improve the nutrition of half-starved internees. Together with Thomas Edgar, Lane Crawford's master baker, he developed a form of bread baked with soya bean residue and lowered sugar content. He also cultivated yeast in the camp to tackle vitamin B2 deficiency, which helped to save the eyesight of numerous malnourished prisoners going blind in desperate circumstances.

The Ma On Shan Marauder

Back in the 1930s, even though the press reports were peppered with a knowing cynicism that often appears unnecessary and churlish in the light of Herklots' academic authority, they did add to the trove of tiger-lore the territory was notching up. A farmer in January 1932 lost three bullocks valued at $130 near the village of Chun Cheng. He found the carcasses up the hills, with deep claw marks on the bodies and their throats torn out. Towards the end of the same year two Indian police in the district of

Ting Kau spotted Stripes by the roadside at 9pm on a brightly moon-lit Saturday night. The report they made was circulated among the stations of the New Territories.

A year later just outside Kowloon City a gardener discovered large paw prints in his grounds. Residents reacted by shutting every door and window, and reinforcing them with extra bolts, locks and iron bars. The beast stalked along the right side of the valley, trampled through several vegetable patches, reached the centre of the village, turned left and disappeared. Pig pens were reinforced with thick wooden bars and wire netting, and villagers took it in turns to man night guards to keep watch for the big cat.

A series of reports starting in 1935 suggest that a particular tiger took residence in the colony. The Ma On Shan Marauder carried away a 70-pound pig from Mr D. Wilson's farm on its debut appearance on the lower slopes of the mountain. It was 20 years after the only tiger officially shot in the territory was dispatched, and the policeman who took credit for that kill, Donald Burlingham, had just announced his retirement as deputy inspector general of the force.

The title "Ma On Shan Marauder" is a liberty taken on my part, and it is best understood as a label that groups a series of reports, rather than a definite single animal. It was never clear that the same tiger was appearing and reappearing but the witnesses and the scribes who recorded the stories would make their call – "the tiger is back...", "another sighting...", "Stripes was seen again..." But it could never be consistent. It was never even certain that there was only one animal. Sometimes the "Marauder" was a pair of tigers, as one early witness thought who reported two sets of footprints near Ma On Shan, one slightly bigger than the other, suggesting a possible mother and offspring duo.

Whether it was one or two, there was something mysterious in the hills that winter and it was large and threatening. A woman was cutting wood at five o'clock in the morning soon after the first livestock raid when she noticed a pair of eyes gazing at her through the thicket. She hurriedly retreated to the village with an awareness that she was being stalked.

News reached the retiring Burlingham and undoubtedly he relished the thought of re-enacting his glory days by bagging a second tiger in Hong Kong. The old hero put together a search party, but he went away empty-handed and into retirement in Britain. When he passed away in the 1950s, his wish was to have his ashes brought back to Tai Po, not far from where he had killed the Sheung Shui tiger in 1915, and where he had spent the happiest years of his life.

As the 1935 hunt went on, three soldiers saw the beast from their car, lit up by their headlamps at around 1 o'clock in the morning near the Kowloon Reservoir. Sergeant-Major W. Wilson, Sergeant B. Eldridge and Corporal G. Bostock were from the East Lancashire regiment and they were on their way back from Kowloon to the military camp at Fanling when they spotted a stealthy animal by the roadside. The spooked feline dashed across the road, revealing its yellow coat with black stripes. It tried to clamber up the roadside embankment, but couldn't get a foothold.

Sergeant Eldridge decided that it was better to move on than to investigate the agitated big cat, so he pressed his foot down on the accelerator. At that moment the tiger slipped down the slope it had tried to climb and leapt right in front of the car. Somehow the soldiers managed to swerve past the predator and drive on.

Just when they thought it was all over, one of them looked back to see the tenacious tiger loping after them. Finally they came across a contingent of Indian policemen, and to their relief they saw the weaponry they were packing. The soldiers recounted the terrifying episode and handed over to the policemen, leaving them to scour the district with their Thompson guns, though nothing came of it.

The Marauder was next seen two days later, on Christmas Eve over near Tsuen Wan. Following another appearance at Shatin the day after Boxing Day, someone stated the obvious: "the tiger seems to be roaming about a good bit."

An unconfirmed report from Lai Chi Kok came through on New Year's Eve and on 2nd January 1936, the Ma On Shan Marauder once again became two animals. The pair were seen by four Indian policemen near Sheung Wun Yiu village, Tai Po. The constables were very near the big cats, within four yards, but before any of them managed to get a gun out, the skittish predators leapt into bushes and vanished. The *Telegraph*, the *China Mail* and the *Daily Press* all recounted the same story.

Lau Ping and Lau Lokum, two "earth coolies" who lived at the Fat Lee Contractors shop in Lai Chi Kok Road, were on their way to a work site at Shing Mun pass when they saw a sleeping tiger by the roadside. The police promptly went out to scour the land. They must have been desperate to find the beast by now.

Three parties, each under a European officer, set out on 11th January to converge from different angles to the spot where the slippery feline was seen complacently napping. They were heavily armed and no doubt in a state of tension and excitement. They scoured the district but at the end of their efforts had nothing to show for it. It seems the tiger only ever revealed itself to those who were not looking for it. It was a Zen tiger – seek me and you will not see me. Chances are, the sly carnivore was watching the hapless humans, perhaps even stalking the hunters.

Shots were fired a week later in Sai Kung when an Indian officer reported a sighting to his sergeant. R.G. Clarke swiftly took a party out to the spot, where they fired blindly into the undergrowth, reaping nothing in return.

Six weeks later at 8:45 in the morning the Marauder was seen just north of Kowloon Tong. Brave villagers who did not want the apex predator near their houses massed together and drove the big cat back into the hills. Elsewhere on that same day women grass-cutters were chased down a hillside. They were saved by the folk wisdom about running downhill from the stumpy-front-legged feline.

After weeks of stories about the Ma On Shan Marauder, the readership, or at least an editor, is struck by a spot of feline fatigue and a discussion is aired on whether the tiger is after all just some wolves. "Stripes" presumably was offended by this and a week later left an unmistakable calling card. A bull lay bleeding to death about a mile and a half from Kowloon Tong police station, with its throat torn away and half its intestines missing.

Just to eliminate any excuse for doubt, the beast left a nice collection of clear footprints around the bovine victim.

That was enough for authorities to put up a $50 reward for anyone who managed to kill the killer. The accounts kept coming in, but they were confusing and perhaps confused. Some saw two; some said the tigers were black, recalling perhaps Caldwell's mysterious blue tiger. Everyone seemed to have a story. Three Europeans, an Indian constable and a Chinese constable all spotted a pair of them on a hillside behind No.1 Kent Road, Kowloon Tong, at about 6:50pm. Then over in Fanling Mr Archer of the Maritime Customs saw "large scraggy beasts, moving quickly and quietly in the real cat manner." Five days later another story came in from the tiger beacon of Tai Mo Shan, this time from two naval officers, Paymaster Commander Steele and Paymaster Lieutenant Osborne of HMS *Capetown*, who had got lost on the misty mountain and had been forced to stay out overnight.

"About five o'clock, or just before dawn, the mist was beginning to lift. We were walking down one of the channels in the side of Tai Mo Shan near a Chinese cemetery when we suddenly and independently caught sight of the tigers," Steele said. Curiously, these too were black, though Steele "had no doubt what they were."

Towards the end of this episode another rumour of a human mauling surfaced from the local Chinese community. It is not clear if the "mauling" was fatal, and none of the papers got to the bottom of it. I suspect that no one had the full picture on the Ma On Shan Marauder by the time the cascade of reports petered out.

Hong Kong man-eater

Mr Winslade was strolling along the catchwater near the Kowloon Reservoir in September 1936 when he came across some unusual-looking animal tracks. The footprints were five and a half inches across and firmly imprinted in thick mud, and there were fifty of them wandering in all directions. He photographed them, and experts pronounced – the tiger was back.

Three days later, five partly devoured carcasses of buffaloes in Sai Kung district added to the dossier of evidence. Water buffaloes around here are built like rhinoceroses. A more modest carnivore would normally leave such walking battle tanks alone. But these were severely mauled, all five of them, and slashing razor-blade claw marks were carved all over the hides of the dead cattle. Sai Kung villagers feared for their remaining livestock, and perhaps for themselves too.

Yet once again the trail went dead. They were ghostly, those tigers.

It took three more months until another sighting, and this time the venue was at Lok Ma Chau village, right on the border with the mainland. When a cow disappeared the first thought was theft, but when someone found the bloodstained remains scattered on a hillside, it was taken as proof the tiger was at large.

Meanwhile news filtered through that more than 60 people in Guangdong had been eaten by tigers that besieged a village. The predators had effectively imposed a curfew. Each afternoon from 1pm the inhabitants locked themselves into their houses and stayed indoors until 5pm. It was the period known as the "feeding time" of the beasts. The district government offered a reward for each tiger killed, but there were no takers, the villagers preferring to abide by the tiger's curfew.

Hong Kong wasn't immune to the man-eaters either.

A dead tiger was found in the bushes in the New Territories and many in the countryside breathed a sigh of relief. It must have been the Kowloon Wanderer or the Ma On Shan Marauder that had so rattled nerves the previous year, or at least that's what a lot of people thought. There is no way of telling when one tiger ends and another begins, or if they overlap, but it turned out that there was still a tiger out there, and it was much worse than the previous ones.

The 1937 Tai Wai Rambler left a brief but devastating legacy. It killed people.

First came a woman near mine No. 7 on the northeast face of Tai Mo Shan. She had been reduced to blood-stained remains, with "nearly the whole of her body missing." Then a man headed up the hill to collect firewood, and was never seen again. Local wisdom left little doubt – he had been carried off and eaten.

At the end of January villagers were still convinced that a man-eater was in the neighbourhood, but once again the trail goes cold and it is no wonder that over in China many people attributed magic powers to the Lord of the Hundred Beasts.

It is quite remarkable that with yearly tiger visits during this period we don't get to hear more of human casualties in Hong Kong. The toll in the mainland during the same period was quite devastating. Harry Caldwell regularly came across villages where dozens of people had been taken – tigers nabbed children from inside their homes and jumped grass-cutters working in groups. There is no doubt that the animals were capable of the cruellest slaughter. But Hongkongers were mostly left intact.

Back in 1915 Goucher and Singh were fatally injured as they were going after the beast, and we know that the King does not like to be provoked or cornered. Other than that, we've come across very few rumours of killings, but many sightings, nonchalant passings and strictly-non-human leftovers. I wonder if the tiger is generally more confident in its home territory. Caldwell's observations make it clear that the tiger prefers to take decisive actions when it feels in control of the situation. A stalking tiger can be spooked by spindly grass-cutters if taken by surprise, though it can make the most audacious raids when it takes command of the environment. In Hong Kong they were visitors, and tiger-lore would say don't mess with the humans, especially in strange lands. However, this did not help the two sadly anonymous Tai Wai villagers who join Goucher and Singh with the rare honour of those killed inside Hong Kong by the Lord of the Hundred Beasts.

To knife a tiger

In 1938 the population of the territory had hit a million and thousands of people were pouring across the border each day to escape the Japanese march southward. As tensions rose, on one Tuesday in February, a Sham Shui Po tiger chased a dog in a vegetable plantation at around 2:30 in the afternoon. The dog got away. An unremarkable account, but let it be noted here that where today there are endless rows of shops and buildings, and relentless traffic in the dense Kowloon hinterland – a wild tiger once chased a dog.

A few weeks after the dog-chasing beast of Sham Shui Po, an eloquent contributor to the *China Mail* explained that as big cat reports had quietened down, and it being a Sunday, he decided to take a hike up in the hills. He was no fool and he knew he should be prepared, so he took with him a seven-inch kitchen knife.

Sure enough, it was good to be ready, because when he reached the rocky upland, alone and armed only with a cooking utensil, he saw "something large" with a heavy body moving downward. Following "pure instinct" he transferred the blade from a back pocket to the inside of his jacket; "fingers of one hand held a firm grip on the handle, the other being in possession of a walking stick."

It is strange he kept his seven-inch blade on the inside of his jacket, as if he didn't want to reveal too early what he was packing. I would have had it out right in front of me, Samurai style, ready to slash. Lucky for our man up the hill, he did not need to reveal his weapon, because the enemy slunk away without even offering a fully confirmed view of its stripes. The intrepid knife hunter was spooked enough to warn his readers with authority – there's something out there, be ready.

There clearly was something out there, but it was far more dangerous than the tiger: it was the Japanese imperial army, the new ruler of Canton, with its eyes on Hong Kong.

Chapter 8

TORA! TORA! TORA!

1940 – 1950

Never mind the tigers, here come the Japanese

Just over a year before Japanese troops shot their way into Hong Kong, a farmer on Tai Mo Shan set out to milk his cow. He found it on the ground bleeding to death with a large chunk taken out of its side. The gory wound looked like the work of a single bite. The villagers had heard spine-chilling growls but no one saw anything.

It was a wild time. A sense of dread hung over Hong Kong, as black and heavy as one of the colony's frequent drenched thunderclouds waiting to burst. Wild dogs ran amok on Hong Kong Island itself, not just in the New Territories where they belonged. They were reported in Shek O, Deep Water Bay, Tai Tam and Pok Fu Lam, killing domestic dogs and howling through the night. Furious villagers had to beat back packs, but the dogs were hungry and grabbed what they could. They took chickens and tore pigs apart.

But the curs had their nemesis, and the Lord of the Hundred Beasts still made its presence felt.

The next tiger appeared in February of the fateful year 1941, or at least signs of its visit were spotted. Pad marks were left on the side of Tai Mo Shan, the territory's highest peak, and so often a beacon for itinerant tigers. Water buffaloes lay dead nearby. Then in March there were spoor marks around the carcass of a deer with part of its back legs ripped off, near the Tai Hang squatters' camp at Jardine's Lookout.

To the rulers of the colony, tigers and packs of dogs were the least of their worries. From the time that the Japanese army had set up a puppet state in Manchuria, where the proud Siberian tiger prowled, the clock was ticking for Hong Kong. The Japanese installed the hostage emperor Puyi in the north, and plotted a steady destructive march southward. The Marco Polo Bridge incident near Beijing in 1937 was taken as a cue for Japan to push on with renewed determination. It was a skirmish between Japanese troops already stationed in northern China, and Chinese forces trying to keep the invaders at bay. Chiang Kai-shek used it to bomb Japanese concessions in Shanghai, while Japan gladly took that on board to smash through the coastal city and onto Nanking where war-crazed troops raped and pillaged on a horrific rampage through the Nationalist capital.

From a vast northern block of territory, pockets of the southern coastline were taken in an archipelago of Japanese force, reaching Canton in 1938, where the new Asian superpower prepared its next move, breathing down the neck of Hong Kong. They told Hong Kong that the entire China coast was on a trade blockade, and the British colony was expected to obey the order.

In good Hong Kong tradition, smugglers worked overtime to funnel 60,000 tons of arms a month into China, while violence raged in the north, sending hundreds of thousands of refugees south. The population of the colony had already reached a million in 1938, and by 1940, 5,000 more people were crossing the border each day. The South China tiger would have looked on in dismay as tens of thousands of fretful and hungry humans set up messy squatter camps on once-quiet hillsides and valleys, lighting fires and stripping woodland of anything left that was useful or edible.

War had already broken out in Europe in 1939, and the British knew their empire was hopelessly overstretched. Expat women and children started being evacuated from Hong Kong in 1940. White ladies and their offspring headed to Australia, while the brown and brownish people were dropped off in Manila, as Japan spluttered anti-European propaganda in the form of the Greater East Asia Co-Prosperity Sphere. By January 1941, British PM Winston Churchill knew there was "not a slightest chance of holding Hong Kong."

The plan was simply to stall the invasion for as many days as possible, to slow down Japan's relentless drive through Southeast Asia, to protect the more important British possession of Singapore. For that purpose two regiments of Canadian infantry were sent to Hong Kong, arriving in November 1941 on what was surely a hopeless mission.

As these troops set foot on the ground the last pre-war tigers were reported at the Peak and Tai Tam. A writer going by the name of Vinjar suggested there may have been two. He said it was well known that tigers were occasionally observed in the New Territories, but that there were no records for the island. In fact the first Hong Kong Island tiger of the century was in 1911, and they kept coming back, as we have seen. Tigers went where they wanted.

Vinjar wondered if a much smaller animal was cause for concern in 1941. The recent total blackout of the colony had a peculiar effect, he wrote. When the lights went out on the Peak, air raid wardens and residents noticed with dismay that large patches of hillside suddenly came into view in a mass of tiny spotlights that glowed on and faded out, in a repeating pulsating illumination. Usually unnoticed by the busy, important and well-lit people of the Peak, thousands of fireflies signalling in unison suddenly took centre-stage in the blackout. Vinjar relaxed after examining the evidence and concluded that the firefly gleam wasn't strong enough to be seen from the cockpit of a Japanese bomber.

Tora! Tora! Tora! was the Japanese battle cry for a surprise attack, an abbreviation of *Totsugeki Raigeki*, meaning lightning attack. *Tora* is also Japanese for tiger, and that is apt as we know that the tiger's favourite mode of attack is the ambush, as was Japan's devastating and vicious raid on Pearl Harbour on 7th December 1941. It was an effective way of bringing the Americans into the war, but it left the US Pacific Fleet crippled, and any hope Hong Kong had that Uncle Sam would sail to the rescue was bombed to smithereens.

When Japanese troops bounded over the Shenzhen River as many a tiger had over the past decades, Hong Kong's coastal defence guns were facing the wrong way. The Japanese, who at that point probably believed their own propaganda about invincibility, blew up the few RAF planes that were on the ground at Kai Tak airport and took complete control of the skies. The British mule-drawn light guns were of little use without air-spotting of troop movements. Japanese artillery on the other hand was consistently accurate thanks to pre-war agents who had mapped everything in Hong Kong to lethal detail on carefree peaceful hikes in happier days.

That left 3,000 rifles guarding the 11-mile Gin Drinkers Line to hold off the invaders for as long as possible. It does not seem like an auspicious name, though I can imagine it was only too accurate. The defence was a set of concrete bunkers and tunnels, snaking high over the ridges of the New Territories. Sections were named after London streets and train stations, and many had the effect of trapping soldiers inside as the Japanese dropped grenades through ventilation holes. It took 48 hours for the Japanese to overrun the peninsula, and for the British command to retreat across the harbour to Hong Kong Island for their last stand.

The leadership cabled London to tell them how hopeless it was, and Churchill, who already knew that, came back on 23rd December to urge "There must however be no thought of surrender... there must be vigorous fighting in the inner defences, and, if need be, from house to house." Two days later the last remnants of the resistance had been pushed to Stanley peninsula and there was nothing to do but surrender.

The invading soldiers went on a rape and massacre rampage. Nurses, doctors and patients were slaughtered at St Stephen's hospital. On Kowloon side, a Dr Li Shu-fan reported that his hospital had treated 10,000 rape victims. People were threaded together with fists pushed through bayonet holes in each other's arms and thrown into the harbour. Others were left strung up in trees.

There followed three and a half years of devastation, during which the Hong Kong population were understandably distracted from tiger sightings. Public services collapsed, most children stopped going to school, and the economy fell apart. Nearly 3,000 non-Chinese enemy nationals were interned at Stanley prison camp in a state of near-starvation, medical neglect, and under harsh discipline that could slip into torture and death at any time. Meanwhile outside the fence an estimated 10,000 civilians, mostly Chinese, were executed by the Japanese. A guerrilla force in the New Territories backed by communist Chinese support made heroic raids on the new occupiers, while some wealthy citizens who had got rich under the British administration changed caps and served the new regime, and others took shelter in the neutral Portuguese colony of Macau. Rumours abounded that the Japanese were releasing deadly snakes in the hills to flush out the guerrilla resistance.

The prisoners' tiger

In the midst of this chaos, in 1942, a tiger appeared at Stanley internment camp. Compared to starvation and torture, the appearance of a tiger seemed a trivial matter to many inmates who dismissed such tales as "preposterous", but author Geoffrey Charles Emerson makes the point that it was something of great interest in an otherwise monotonous existence.

There is a good account of it in George Wright-Nooth's diary, published under the title *Prisoner of The Turnip Heads*.

> "Last night Langston and Dalziel, who were sleeping outside at the back of the bungalow, were woken up at about 5:00am by snarls and growls. Langston… got up to have a look. He went to the edge of the garden and looked down the slope to the wire fence. There Dalziel saw him leap in the air and fly back into the boiler room, shouting "There's a tiger down there"… Next morning, on being told the story we were inclined to laugh."

The inmates were understandably nervous about a marauding tiger because they slept crammed together in derelict buildings that had no

He went to the edge of the garden and looked down the slope...

windows or doors. On 1ˢᵗ June, 1942, Wright-Nooth recorded: "Early this morning there was much activity on the hill behind the camp which was being searched by parties of Chinese and Indian police under caps... One of the Chinese supervisors told me that an Indian policeman had been mauled by a tiger at about 2.00am."

Two tiger guards were appointed, but their weaponry was severely limited. One had a gong, the other a gardening fork. It didn't make much difference to the troubled nights of the sleepless inmates: "As usual we all slept outside. At about 3am I heard Colin say, "Geoffrey! Don't move, there's a TIGER eating a bone behind your bed!" On that occasion the tiger turned out to be a coat, and the 'bone' was a pillow.

Eventually a real hunting party, armed with real weapons, returned with a real 240-pound carcass of a six foot long, three foot high, male tiger killed just outside the camp. The shooter was named Rur Singh, an Indian police constable. Some in the party insisted it wasn't the only tiger out there, as they had seen a mate and two cubs escape the shooters.

Butcher B.W. Bradbury, a former worker at the Dairy Farm Company in Pok Fu Lam, where 1,900 cows had been kept before the war, was taken out of the prison to skin the prize. Apparently he was the most unpopular man at the camp, according to Wright-Nooth, though we don't find out why. The stuffed trophy was taken to the city where war-weary people could view it for a distraction from the ordinary horrors of war. The meat was taken by a Japanese officer and given to officials at the Hong Kong Race Club who made a feast out of it. The *Hong Kong News* reported that it was as "tender and delicious as beef."

Some people believed that the tiger had escaped from a circus that happened to be in Hong Kong when the Japanese invaded; others said it had come down from China and swum the harbour. The circus theory remains popular today, but there isn't much information about a circus in town at the time of the Japanese invasion. Discussion on the *Gwulo* online historical forum has brought up a Philippine circus that some people recall.

Certainly a circus could be the explanation, but again you would have to ask if, considering the lack of clarity on the circus, that explanation is necessarily simpler than a wild tiger, or possibly four of them, wandering through the chaos of war-ravaged southern China looking for food and shelter and ending up at Hong Kong? As we have seen, the reports of wild tigers continued to surface through the period before the war, and as we will see, will continue to do so afterwards. So do we need a circus to "understand" the Stanley Tiger?

It so happened that an expert was at hand.

Geoffrey Herklots was interned at the camp at the time of the tiger appearance. He dryly recalled years later that Taiwanese prison guards had got excited about the beast, and for a while it was dangerous walking about the place in the evening as you risked being accidentally shot by a would-be tiger hunter. Herklots admitted that he wasn't convinced by the pug marks that were first shown to him, but when he saw the photograph of the dead tiger he scoffed at the stories of the circus escapee, noting: "It is strange how loath people are to believe that tigers do visit the Colony and occasionally swim the harbour and visit the Island."

The skin of the Stanley tiger is still on display today at the Tin Hau temple next to Stanley Plaza. It is a big dark shaggy brown thing, ragged at the edges and dirty-looking. Its colouring could be the result of immersion in decades of thick incense smoke. It looked more like a bear skin to me than a tiger's, but if you look closely you can see stripes. Tin Hau is the fishermen's goddess, but probably doesn't mind sharing a shrine with a fearsome tiger skin. After all, the tiger is an awesome display of nature's power, as is the sea and the wonders inside of it, and at least for some moments the tiger is a marine mammal as it swims across sea channels in search of riches.

I asked the lady sitting outside the temple welcoming visitors if she knew about the tiger. "Yes," she said, "in Stanley, came from China, very scary," nodding knowingly. "Had there been any others?" I asked. She laughed at my question. "Oh no," she said emphatically, "we'd be dead if there were," shuddering at the thought, as if tigers were more dangerous than the Japanese invasion.

Amoy tiger bait
Over the border in Japanese-occupied China there were plenty of tigers. Eugene Yu-Wei Chen was five or six years old when he was in Xiamen, South China tiger country, under the Japanese occupation. Conditions were harsh, with little to eat. The Japanese took all the best rice from storehouses, leaving locals with scraps of grain that crumbled to dust when pressed between thumb and forefinger. Years later his wife, American writer Nicki Chen, recounted the story he told.

The occupiers also took livestock – pigs, chickens and goats – and Chinese farmers were forced ever further into mountain forests in search of food. They were pushed into tiger country.

With humans and tigers competing for the same dwindling stock of prey, even as people pushed up into the hills, tigers were coming down to the plains. Writing in her blog *Behind the Story*, Chen tells of two tigers that hit the Fujian coast at Xiamen, swimming across the strait to Amoy Island where they attacked a woman. The victim's husband managed to shoot one of the tigers, but the other one got away. Sadly the wounded lady died before help could reach her.

Japanese soldiers arrived at the scene and immediately banned the husband from retrieving the body of his wife lying in the street. They wanted to keep her there as bait to lure the second tiger back.

It worked. The tiger returned and the Japanese got it. They butchered the two carcasses, keeping their hearts, livers and pelts, and they sold off the rest of the meat to the hungry Chinese population.

Who let the cats back in?
The Japanese finally surrendered after the atomic bombings of Hiroshima and Nagasaki in August 1945. They couldn't leave Hong Kong immediately because they were needed to patrol the streets. The only other organised force available was a group of about seven hundred triads

who had been allowed to run gambling dens under the occupation in exchange for keeping order.

A row ensued at conference tables around the world about the future of Hong Kong, with the Americans supporting the idea of handing the colony back to China. But which China? The wily Brits stalled, as Admiral Harcourt sailed in to re-establish the badly damaged imperial prestige.

His staff were appalled at the mess the Japanese had left: "untidiness and filth was the general rule. Bottles of apple wine and beer lie around, some half full. The paintwork is shabby... the ropes are fifth-rate," Lieutenant John Gibson wrote. Some 30 to 40 thousand "coolies" were employed to clear up the mess.

Eight months of post-war military rule eventually gave way to a British civil administration on 1st May 1946, and perhaps taking a liking to the newly cleaned up Hong Kong, tigers came back with a vengeance through the remaining years of the decade.

The press reported at least ten tiger appearances from October 1946 to the end of 1949, during which time dozens of cows, pigs and dogs were torn apart, tiger meat appeared on market stalls, and at least one human was mauled. This is the most intensive period for tiger reports in the brief survey that I have made. This was also the period that a civil war raged in China, as battle-hardened and heavily-armed Communist guerrillas pushed the Nationalists over every valley and hill and eventually into the sea. Human enemies were the top priority of the communists, but it would not be long until the same victorious guerrilla forces would have the time and space to train their weapons on a four-legged enemy of the people.

Once again the big-cat-beacon that is Tai Mo Shan sets the scene for the first post-war tiger. Villagers saw footprints on the flanks of the mountain and reported a prowler to the authorities. The published account suggests Hong Kong yet again had a new batch of editors who had not studied the pre-war history of the tiger in the territory. You can almost see an arched eyebrow as an amused hack stabbed out the letters on his typewriter, sleeves rolled, loose tie dangling from his neck like a disused noose, tattered homburg tipped at an angle, and a cigarette hanging from the corner of his mouth: "As if armed gangsters, money sharks, black marketeers and other rats, both metaphorical and literal, weren't enough, the Colony of Hong Kong is now blessed with a tiger, if the village folk of Tsun Wan, at the foot of Tai Mo Shan, are to be believed."

The village folk at the foot of Tai Mo Shan did not need convincing. They put together a hunting party and went scouring the hills. No doubt some people took the fact that they returned with a boar rather than a big cat as proof that there was no tiger. The villagers knew though. The Lord of the Hundred Beasts was back, if ever he had left.

Two weeks later, probably the same wit wrote: "Wash Amah's elder brother's youngest son arrived home much excited an evening or so back to report that the carcass of a tiger was on sale in one of the side-streets of the Central District." Despite the tongue-in-cheek scepticism, the reporter rushed to Central Market to investigate the claim. Unfortunately he was too late to buy any tiger steak, but he saw a skeleton, he said. He quizzed the vendor on where the carcass came from, but the butcher was reluctant to talk, suggesting only that it may have been caught in the New Territories. The vendor skulked away before answering further questions about exactly where it had been caught or by whom.

In the spring of 1947 more tiger meat was for sale at Tai Po Market. A villager of Sum Chung village near Tai Mo Shan caught a cub and sold it to a vendor for $200. The delicacy quickly sold out at $16 per catty on a stall at Tsing Yuen Street.

Hong Kong's tiger battles

In the last two years of the 1940s there were so many tiger reports that they almost became humdrum. A human-animal conflict was taking place in the small territory that was perhaps a minor reflection of the real man-tiger war that would play out in the mainland over the following twenty years.

The Lai Chi Wo tiger slew a cow, a pig and a dog in April, and several months after that the Tao Fung Shan tiger slaughtered a water buffalo at Wong Chuk Yeung village. Police said no-one had told them anything about a big cat. The villagers took matters into their own hands and set out to hunt down the beast.

On New Year's Day 1948, it was the police themselves who reported a tiger. Sub-Inspector G.J. Perkins, police armourer, was able to confirm that the tiger seen in the New Territories was "not a figment of imagination." He saw it from about 300 yards away, creeping about in the grass before clearly showing itself. "It was a big thing, weighing about 300 catties," he estimated. The *SCMP* said that Perkins had taken a shot near Lin Ma Hang, and possibly wounded it. Two small tigers were seen to retreat across the border into Chinese territory a day later.

The Tai Wai Chuen tiger must have been a heavy hitter too. Frantic pig squealing attracted the attention of a night watchman at 2am. He shone his torch out to the source of the blood-curdling screams and there saw a tiger with a pig in its jaws, "trotting towards the hillside." An animal that trots with a pig in its jaws is not an animal to mess with.

But mess with them we did. More tiger meat was on sale at a Hong Kong market in mid-January. Someone spotted the exotic item at Sha Tau Kok on a Wednesday at 5pm. The skin had already been sold earlier to a village resident.

The tigers would not give up either.

A farmer lost another pig two weeks later. Ng Yung saw his 200-catty porker being dragged away by a big cat in the direction of the railway tunnel. He was so terrified that he fainted. Villagers found what was left of the pig near the tunnel entrance the next morning, and set out with their dogs to continue the battle against the feline invader.

Then there were three tigers roaming the hills of Ta Kwu Ling near the frontier with warring China. They left behind them only the intestines and bones of a pig nearby. The tigers of southern China must have known they were onto a good thing in Hong Kong, slipping past the civil-war battle lines of Guangdong and Fujian.

Two more pigs disappeared in the night near Tai Wai village in March 1948. The farmer heard the squealing but was too afraid to look. The next morning they found blood stains near a railway track, intestines scattered on the hillside, and 23 tiger paw prints on the ground.

As Hong Kong was seeing a spike in tiger activities, the species carried on its usual shenanigans in its homeland. In Fujian, the epicentre of South China tiger territory, some 100 people had been killed by the predator in the year leading to the first months of 1948. Over in Guilin, the discovery of a mutilated body at the city gate provoked the formation of armed guards assigned to track down and kill man-eaters.

Back in Hong Kong another unremarkable sighting occurred on a hillside at midnight. A villager thought he had disturbed a thief and pointed a flashlight towards the commotion, only to be rewarded with the sight of a tiger creeping away.

At the end of a bumper year for tiger sightings, the *SCMP* drops a bombshell. A tiger was shot and killed in the New Territories. It was slightly larger than an Alsatian dog, so it wasn't fully grown. It was strapped onto the front of a jeep and driven to Hong Kong Island. It is remarkable that this tiger has not entered the canon of Hong Kong tiger lore, which only amounts to two in any case, the 1915 and 1942 tigers.

There were further reports in the final year of the decade, including one near Tsuen Wan in May, and then a few days later at the Fanling golf course. Another report on spoors in July starts with the words: "Inevitably, as has been the case every winter, farmers have found footprints of a tiger in their paddy fields at Shatin". The following day a pregnant cow had its stomach torn open and two months later cowherds in Sai Kung observed a tiger watching their livestock.

There had never been so many tiger reports filed in Hong Kong one after another in such quick succession.

A few thousand miles to the north, a momentous event was taking place. Chairman Mao – who had once led a ragged band of guerrillas in the mountainous badlands – stood up on the Gate of Heavenly Peace in the capital and declared the new People's Republic of China. Having come out of the wilderness to overcome the odds, conquer their enemies, and take the nation, the new regime now set out to tame the wilderness itself.

At that time there were still thousands of South China tigers, and in the coming years the beasts once revered as divine would be identified as vermin. Veteran fighters would gain a new legitimate target to set their sights on.

Falling back on generations of myth-making, many Fujianese people would come to believe that their old foe, the man-eaters, started to disappear within a few years of the new regime because harmony and order had been restored after 'liberation.' In truth, modern weapons of war had more to do with it.

The establishment of Communism in the mainland swelled refugee numbers in Hong Kong to two million toward the end of the decade. The government preferred the term 'squatters' for the new arrivals, as it freed the administration from obligations associated with the word 'refugee'. As it was, they offered the migrants four pegs in a rectangle of land. The rest was up to the incomers to make of it what they could with the help of their relatives, friends and triad societies.

The territory wasn't exactly filling up, but of course at that time they didn't pile flats on top of each other 50 or 60 floors high as they would later. Inevitably human occupation was spreading outwards across the colony. Tigers before this period had more options when they wanted to avoid humans. They could quickly scamper away from village settlements and the outskirts of suburbia to disappear into the ragged and scratty bush, or melt into the background on empty open hills and drop down into hidden gullies. But squatter camps were filling up the available space and though close encounters between tigers and people were rare through the first half of the century, one man got closer than usual just after the establishment of the People's Republic in 1949.

Ten days after Mao stood up to make his famous declaration on the Gate of Heavenly Peace, a truck driver saw a tiger up in the New Territories heading towards Lion Rock. Then all was quiet for a few weeks, until 4th December when a man turned up at a hospital badly mauled.

The 31-year-old Ng Yung was hunting boar with companions on the hillsides above Shatin. They had with them two dogs that eagerly led the way. When one of the hounds started barking fiercely, Ng rushed to the scene to find the dog locked in battle with a tiger cub. The hunter either wanted to rescue his dog, or saw this as a golden opportunity to bag a great prize alive, or possibly both. Instead of using his gun, he waded into the brawl and grabbed the tiger by the neck.

They said it was a cub, which brings to mind something cute and perhaps a bit bigger than a cat. But this animal was hefty enough to knock Ng's front teeth out. Tigers box, they swing punches with powerful paws. The gloves are off when they fight. Razor-blade claws are unsheathed. Ng had flesh torn from his thighs and arms.

When his hunting companions caught up, the battle-scarred Ng was still holding onto his vicious and thrashing prey. Unable to get a clear shot, the late-comers joined the fight wielding their rifle butts, trying to kill the animal by staving in its head. Pain from Ng's injuries got the better of him and he was forced to let go. The bewildered feline disappeared into the undergrowth and narrowly escaped being the last tiger killed in Hong Kong. Ng was carted off in an ambulance to be hospitalised for ten days. His dog died.

Chapter 9

THE ROCK AND ROAR YEARS

After 1950

War against tigers

At the beginning of the 1950s there were an estimated 4,000 South China tigers roaming the wild, mainly concentrated in the four provinces of Fujian, Jiangxi, Hunan and Guangdong. That is more than today's total estimated global wild tiger population in a geographic range that stretches from the Indian and Bangladeshi Sundarbans across to eastern Siberia and down as far as Sumatra. By 1961 the estimated population had dropped to 1,000. The events of the decade in between dealt a critical blow to the South China tiger.

Sightings in Hong Kong dropped off dramatically compared to the five years that followed the war, but began early in the new decade with a report of two in the winter of 1950, including one "believed very large". They were witnessed by several villagers at the Lin Ma Hang district. The local chief inspector led a search party backed up with three rifles and a Winchester. They found a cave on a hillside that looked promising, but failed to track down the beasts.

It was yet another frustrating search for a member of the elusive species that seems to have the power to melt into the landscape whenever people are looking for it. But the all-too-familiar calling cards were there to be seen. A mangled, half-eaten cow lay on the brink of a cliff by a small stream. Nearby another gored carcass of a bovine was left on the ground and by the side of that was a dead calf. The search continued, but the story petered out.

This was a period of immense change in and around Hong Kong. A new war was being fought in the region, on the Korean peninsula. The war had a direct effect on Hong Kong, as trade embargoes imposed on China for their intervention in North Korea were seriously hobbling the economy of the territory. At the same time the British colonial overlords were struggling to maintain a good relationship with the new global superpower, the United States. Even though the Brits and the Americans, along with the United Nations, cooperated in Korea to push back against the Northern Communist onslaught, there were huge differences in attitude toward Beijing, the mighty new backer of Pyongyang. The Americans at that time were still holding out for a Nationalist takeover of mainland China, while Britain was among the first countries to acknowledge the new People's Republic of China. It was a fraught relationship as the United States turned their consulate in Hong Kong into the biggest CIA base abroad.

How did all this affect the tigers?

In Korea, geopolitics had already helped to push the tiger over the brink of existence. The Japanese upper classes and the colonial leadership had long sought name and glory in chasing down Korean tigers to send back as trophies to the homeland. Hong Kong newspapers reported on their exploits in gossipy glamour columns, just as they would continue to do so on British royal hunting parties in India into the 1960s.

"Another report just to hand tells of a thrilling adventure experience recently with a big tiger by two Japanese hunters living at Muan," the *Hong Kong Telegraph* breathlessly reported in March 1913. It went into detail that involved chases, near misses, roaring counter-attacks and a final bullet that "entered the brain of the animal through the right eye" causing it to drop dead instantly. The skin was bought jointly by the Japanese Municipal Office and Chamber of Commerce to be presented to Count Terauchi, Governor of Korea.

Two years later we hear of three Japanese hunters who went up a mountain. They saw three tigers at once and fired simultaneously. One was shot dead on the spot, another was wounded and a third escaped unhurt. A chap called Ono went chasing after the injured one only to be outwitted by the beast that pounced from behind and bit him on the back of the head. Ono grappled for his life and managed to stick the muzzle of his gun into the mouth of the raging predator and blow its brains out.

The last tiger of Korea was killed only six years after that description, in 1921, according to the *Seoul Times*, citing a Japanese book published in 2009. That one was also killed by a Japanese, an aristocrat from the Imperial Household, with the aid of hundreds of local villagers who participated as tiger chasers. It is always difficult to pinpoint the last of a population on its way to extinction, and there are other sporadic reports reaching into the 1940s, but it's pretty safe to say that the Korean cats were gone before the South China variety were annihilated.

In Korea, it is reasonable to say that Japanese invaders on their self-assigned historical geopolitical mission bore at least some responsibility for the demise of the revered regal feline. They ruled the land, the environment was in their hands, and on their watch one of the most magnificent animals of the ecosystem was exterminated.

In China it was the Communist Party that took charge of the land, and led the onslaught on tigers. As soon as the Party founded the People's Republic, the new state was immediately facing existential threats. It faced them externally, lacking Soviet support, and staring into the face of radical anti-leftist fundamentalism from the United States, backed up by their fortified Hong Kong intelligence base. It faced them at home, mostly in the form of poverty, as the Party saw it. A strong home was needed to head off the outside threats.

The country poured millions of soldiers into North Korea in 1950 to face down an international anti-communist alliance led by the mighty United States. They helped to push the war down to the southern tip of Korea and fought tooth and nail back up to the Chinese border, then back down to the 38th parallel, where it had all begun. You shouldn't do that on an empty stomach, though undoubtedly hundreds of thousands of their soldiers did.

The fight against poverty, especially in the face of war, was both an ideological and a strategic necessity for China. Every possible means of improving the productivity of the land had to be looked at. That is when tigers came into the sights of the new leaders of the land. Not only were the ferocious carnivores preventing farmers from accessing good land, wildlife was also a commodity that served the economic needs of the people. Predator control campaigns were set up by officials in the 1950s, including the *Dahu Yundong* Kill the Tiger Movement, whose slogan was *Dahu, Chuhai:* Kill the Tiger, Banish Evil. US researcher Chris Coggins, who met some of the last members of the *Dahu* campaigns many years later, describes the Party's attitude to the predators as a commitment to the "permanent removal" of the tiger in an ideological war against nature.

As it happened, following 20 years of civil war, some 15 years of Japanese invasion, and a bloody march into the Korean War, lots of people in China were armed. It was a militarised society, and teams of ex-soldiers, hunters and galvanised peasantry were on hand to carry out their patriotic and ideological duties armed with crossbows, muzzle-loaders, machine guns and grenades. The days were numbered for the South China tiger.

The beast of Fierce Ghost Bridge

Without direct knowledge of the formation of anti-tiger squads in mainland China, it is doubtful that tiger watchers in Hong Kong realised they were encountering some of the last tigers to enter the territory, indeed the last tigers in the history of Hong Kong. Even the most eminent biologist of Hong Kong, Geoffrey Herklots, published a book in 1951 – *The Hong Kong Countryside* – which stated as a matter of fact that tiger visits to the colony were a yearly occurrence. That fits with our records, but he did not, nor could he, warn of or predict the coming collapse of the South China tiger.

So in 1951 and 1952 when tigers left their gory calling cards there were no pleas for conservation, no calls to save the tiger. The first attack was on a pig near the border with the mainland. A year later a farmer found his buffalo dead and half-eaten on a hillside grazing ground on Lao Shi Shan, near Wong Nai Tau village. He went to inform the police and then a village group armed with shotguns and spears headed up into the hills to hunt their quarry.

Another attack came days later, this time near Wong Chuk Shan village in Sai Kung district. Farmer Chung had left several water buffaloes out to graze when he heard a stampede. He discovered one buffalo left dead and half-eaten. The killer had stamped its massive footprints all around the carcass. There was a general consensus that it was the same beast that had eaten the other half-buffalo at Lao Shi Shan a few days earlier. When the *China Mail* contacted Sai Kung police on the new report, the constabulary hadn't heard anything, which shows that the police and press reports could only ever be partial. Not every farmer confronted by a tiger thinks informing the police, or the press, is a priority.

The next report would take another three years to reach publication, with the clock relentlessly ticking for Stripes in Hong Kong. During this time the human population was pushing up, and the changing economy was transforming the landscape. The Shek Kip Mei Christmas Day fire left 50,000 people homeless in 1953, destroying one of the territory's biggest shanty towns, as the very land the tigers roamed was being tamed, sealed and reconstructed.

By the time the Korean War ended in the same year, imports to the territory had been choked by the UN and US embargoes for several years. But what Hong Kong cannot buy, Hong Kong makes, and there was a good source of investment to build much-needed factories. During the 1940s and 50s, in addition to the hundreds of thousands of impoverished refugees from the mainland, the city saw an influx of Shanghai entrepreneurs escaping, with cash, from the new Communist regime. This group shrugged off the drop in trade and the depressed economy, and Hong Kong's manufacturing phase took off with factories springing up all around the cheaper outer districts of the colony. With the growth in population and the rise of manufacturing, the landscape of the New Territories was transforming into something that would have been unrecognisable to the local militia of the old walled villages that first defended their land from British colonialists only five decades earlier. It also looked different to the itinerant tigers who wandered over so regularly.

The next "tiger" was relegated to quotation marks in the 1955 report in the *China Mail* that described a fruitless search for the predator. It appeared at Clear Water Bay Road near Cemetery Hill. An 82-year-old grandmother called Chek Yew-lan was startled by the huge animal, resembling a tiger, prowling around her garden at 4:30am. She raised the alarm and, with her Cemetery Hill phantom, set off the latest round of tiger/no-tiger arguments.

When her grandson found dozens of footprints, Army Lieutenant L. Boyes took a look, counted 20, measured them at over 5 inches across, and pronounced: "They could not have been made by any other animal than a tiger. Either that or they were planted there as a joke." Despite the presence of the army official, the police at first told the press that no one had bothered to call them.

Doubters took the platform the following day when an *SCMP* reporter decided that the paw-like marks were too close together for a tiger, could have been weeks old, and no shrubs had been flattened nearby as you would expect. We don't know what qualifications the reporter had that earned him expert status.

Something had definitely spooked the dogs. A nephew, Tam Yee, employed by the Public Works Department, said his two watchdogs always bark when strangers approach the house. On this night they suppressed their instincts to blast aggressive, deafening barks, instead growling in alarm, fear and angry defeat. This recalls the hapless hunter who took a dog as tiger bait up the Guangdong mountains 40 years earlier to bait a man-eater he planned to shoot. Hunter and dog knew the tiger was at large as they heard its roars. But the canny dog survived the night by keeping dead silent, so maddening the hunter he was tempted to shoot the selfish cur in the morning. Yee's dogs retreated down the garden in the face of the Cemetery Hill phantom, until they backed into the house door with a bang, waking up Grandma Chek.

Another expert came to check the prints. Mr Wong Bon of the Hong Kong Gun Club decided that the spoors could have been those of a tiger or a leopard. He must have read Herklots's *The Hong Kong Countryside* as what he said was straight out of the book. He noted that it was unusual for tigers to cross the border in summer, because "they usually swim across Mirs Bay to the New Territories in winter when there is not enough food to be found on the other side of the border."

The following year the tensions of a city packed with both Nationalist activists and Communist sympathisers burst into a wave of violence that once again put the excitement and the dangers of tigers in perspective. Mobs went on the rampage in Kowloon after a resettlement officer ordered the removal of some nationalist flags at one of the new government housing blocks that were built following the Shek Kip Mei fire. Violence spread from Tsuen Wan to Mong Kok, shops were looted, communist-owned factories were attacked; a full-scale riot kicked off. The Swiss consul's wife was burned to death, along with her driver, when their car was set on fire. The army was called in and instructed to fire without hesitation. Some 59 people lost their lives, 44 of them to troops, and 15 at the hand of the rioters. Later, four people were convicted of murder and sentenced to death.

An inquiry blamed poor conditions, low wages and a lack of representation, and noted that triad groups took the opportunity to settle old scores in the chaos. Reformers pushed for democracy while the Colonial Office pronounced that "there was no general demand or need for the introduction of an elected element into the Legislative Council." Meanwhile the cheap labour and poor working conditions of Hong Kong's growing textile mills were threatening the livelihoods of

British mill workers in the industrial north of the UK. With the colony's 12-hour shifts, seven days a week, there was little that could be done to prevent the flooding of markets by cheap Hong Kong products. The world was changing rapidly, the landscape was being re-sculpted with global consequences, as humans proliferated everywhere and South China's tiger country was slipping off the face of the planet.

Three years after the Cemetery Hill phantom, another tiger appeared like an apparition. For some this would be the last tiger of Hong Kong.

A 23-year-old woman saw a tiger sleeping in bushes on a hilltop around Tai Po on a Tuesday afternoon. Lee Ping-kui of Shun Pun Chung village was chopping firewood with three other women when she witnessed the six-foot feline with black and brown stripes down its back. The 35-year-old Ng King-ho also saw it from about 100 yards before the group ran for their lives.

The next day the women led a police party back to the spot but the searchers were left unimpressed when the women failed to find the exact location the animal had appeared. Around the same time, A.T. Lee of Tai Po Kau said his two children complained that the dogs in their bedroom had been scratching and whining all night. He also said he found footmarks on a hillside, as well as indentations in the soil and scratches on the ground. Originally he had assumed the marks in the soil were made by his big dog, but he changed his mind when he heard the wood collectors' story.

A second, armed, group went on an extensive search around Tai Po. It started from the police station at 10am and finished at 5pm. They came back empty-handed and not a single paw mark or any other trace of tiger was found.

This could have been the last tiger of Hong Kong, and it is a frustratingly fleeting report, amounting to two sketchy observations, and unverified marks on the ground retrospectively attributed to a tiger. But two details make the story better.

The first is that the wood gatherers saw the tiger near Man Kwai Kiu, translated as "Fierce Ghost Bridge". The police took it seriously enough

The wood gatherers saw the tiger near Man Kwai Kiu,
translated as "Fierce Ghost Bridge"

to go searching for the animal. Perhaps it was a quiet time for the Tai Po constabulary, and one of those lovely dry sunny days you can get in winter in Hong Kong, perfect for a hike. They came back without a scrap of evidence, no more than you would get in an average haunting. Perhaps this allows us to conclude that Hong Kong's last tiger, the Beast of Fierce Ghost Bridge, may well have been a spectre.

The other aspect of the story is that Fierce Ghost Bridge was in the district of Tai Po.

This is where the British raised their flag in 1899 at a fitful and violence-tinged official ceremony that marked their acquisition of the fiercely independent New Territories. An organised militia of village guards had greeted the flag bearers with locally-forged firearms. They had been no match for British troops backed by a gunboat and Maxim machine-guns. In the past this place was written with the Chinese characters for "Tai", meaning big or great, and "Po", which means step. Today a different character is used for "Po", but one reading of the old characters would be "big step." A local legend has it that the name "big step" derived from the district's reputation as tiger country. Travellers were advised to take big steps when they passed through the land, to minimise a chance encounter with a large, intimidating, striped marauder.

How fitting that the last tiger of Hong Kong revisited its ancestors' old stomping ground, a place so feared that people named it "Big Step" in warning and reverence for the Lord of the Hundred Beasts. And that this was the site of the last stand of the local indigenous resistance to the scheming dealers of London and Beijing. No matter how anyone felt about the politics, the acquisition of Hong Kong by Britain was the beginning of the end of Old China, an ancient world where the tiger competed with the hairless monkey for its place at the ecological apex. Specifically, this apparition occurred at a place called "Fierce Ghost Bridge," as if in warning perhaps that what humans have done to the South China tiger will always come back to haunt us.

The end.

The last tigers of South China

Of course it wasn't the end.

There were still an estimated 1,000 South China tigers in 1961. That number allows for further possibilities in Hong Kong in the 1960s, even if it was a huge drop from the 4,000 of the decade before.

The population crash was completely by design. The *Dahu Yundong* kill-the-tiger movement went on throughout the 1950s but at the start of the new Republic's land reforms, it was not the tigers that they first went for. It was the boars and feral cattle.

As soon as the new state was established, farmers directed by Party-led reforms sowed crops further afield and deeper into previously untamed lands. Wild boar and wandering cattle on the one hand were pushed out further to the periphery, and on the other hand saw great opportunity and started raiding the tasty pickings on new farmland. This defeated the object of expanding agricultural land to increase productivity. The solution seemed simple: the thieves had to be killed.

In Hunan province, the Central-Southern Military and Political Committee issued an invitation to hunters from all over the country to come to Hunan to kill boar and cattle. It is significant that it was the military and political committee that was directing agricultural policy, not an agricultural committee. From the experiences of soldiers and political campaigners it seemed logical that killing wild boar and cattle, the crop thieves, would improve farming productivity in Hunan.

This turned out to be a huge mistake because in taking out the boar and cattle the committee provoked a much fiercer, more dangerous beast. In the uneasy ecological balance that had more-or-less held for hundreds of years, boar and cattle had been doing humans and their domesticated livestock a great service much of the time, as a buffer against the top predator of the system. By depleting that stock, the hairless monkeys had inadvertently put themselves and their livestock in the front line. Reports of tiger confrontations escalated as the hunting teams successfully brought down the boar and cattle populations. It soon became clear that the hunters needed to change their target to a much more dangerous one. What followed in Hunan, according to a 2008 article in state media journal *Legal Weekly*, was a war between humans and tigers.

That war started around 1952, according to the article published in the mainland Chinese press. Just as Hong Kong has poured millions of tonnes of concrete into the sea in reclamation projects, so the taming of the wilderness, and the clearance of tigers, in southern China was termed a "reclamation" of land.

The tigers did not easily concede defeat. The *Hunan Forestry Journal* documented dozens of emergency reports across the province, including tiger encroachments to the biggest city, Changsha, by 1955. The war went on for about a decade and according to journalist Mo Yabo, some 2,000 people were killed, and tens of thousands of livestock were stolen by tigers. The price the tigers paid was much higher, of course, the catastrophic collapse of their population. They lost the war.

Once the target had shifted to the big cats, the authorities saw an ideal opportunity to further the wealth of the People's Republic by selling skins abroad and medicinal parts at home. The government set up hundreds of "foreign trade bureaus" in remote hill stations to collect the pelts. There was an official average of 400 per year in the first half of the 1950s, and this number decreased to an average of 152 for the period 1961 to 1965. Today the thought of 152 pelts a year exported from wild Chinese tigers is astonishing. The official count continued to the early 1970s when 1-2 a year were still logged.

Much lauded tiger teams notched up their kills. By the 1960s Hunanese squads had liquidated 647 South China tigers. That accounted for 88 per cent of all historical records of tiger killings in the province. There was glory to be had, but competition was fierce with many wanting a share. Yanling county, for example, had 427 hunting teams in 1954. Between them there were 25 tiger kills, one tiger per 17 squads. Inevitably certain individuals gained fame. Zhong Yongtai of Yanling county was credited with 11 tiger kills and an astounding 46,900 wild boar and other beasts. That kind of figure is a timely reminder of the Great Leap Forward effect – a movement that was only three years off and credited with the death by starvation of 20 million people due largely to false reporting of farming productivity by local cadre keen to impress Beijing bosses. The 11 tigers though seem more plausible.

Fellow Hunanese hunter Chen Changkui was credited with 12 kills, including three in one day, on the day his first son was born. He kept a five-inch tooth of a tiger as a souvenir, one that he believed belonged to the "Tiger King".

Another county, Leiyang, had a huge tiger problem. More than 120 people were killed in 1952, including 32 people eaten in one day. Thousands of domestic animals were taken. The local magistrate, a 31-year-old leader called Yang Zezhi, brought together military representatives and professional hunters to hold a "tiger convention". From the crack squad they put together, hunter Chen Qifang rose up to gain fame and claim hero status.

Chen's quest against the big cats was personal. He lost a grandson in 1952 after asking the 14-year-old to go out to dig sweet potatoes. When the boy didn't return after dark, the family went out to search for him, but only found one shoe and the paw prints of a tiger. Chen immediately formed a squad of three with his two sons, and went out fuelled by revenge. Within three years his team had grown to 50 men using traps, crossbows, shotguns, snares and explosives. They hunted beasts deep into the mountains and became known throughout the region as the best tiger killing squad. They were even called to Chairman Mao's home village to track what was said to be a 660-pound monster man-eater.

Some 168 tigers were killed in seven years in Leiyang, and Chen was credited with the killing of 138 of them at an average of one every ten days. News of his prowess reached the hallowed political elite of Beijing and Chen was invited for an audience with Premier Zhou Enlai in 1957, earning himself the accolade "King of the Tiger Slayers".

Another tiger-slaying hero was a man called Mao Piao, also known as Mao Laohu Duizhang, "Mao the Tiger Team Captain", who led a squad of more than 30 former revolutionary guerrillas in the campaign against big cats. When Chris Coggins met him in the 1990s, Mao told him of one hunt in 1956 that went on for more than three months without result as the team suffered increasing pressure from the government. When they finally found a tiger they shot it in the leg and then lost track of it. The squad blindly lobbed grenades in the general direction they thought it had gone, and finally found a dead female that was pregnant with two cubs.

The hundred tiger village

By the late 1950s the South China tigers were under severe pressure. They were forced ever closer to their human enemies, and sometimes acted in unusual ways. One such event resulted in the "hundred tiger village".

It was September 1957 when a hamlet of 80 people found themselves besieged by an army of tigers in the middle of the afternoon. The first sign of it was when the cows all rushed back from the hills and entered the village, and then the dogs went completely silent. Terrified villagers understood tigers were about and came out beating their gongs and screaming oaths. In the past such flimsy techniques had worked, but not on this occasion when the tigers refused to disperse. Instead, in an extraordinary account of tiger behaviour, more and more were gathering to join the siege until there were over a hundred surrounding the village.

Tigers do not work in teams. They tend to avoid each other. There was even a local saying that a mountain cannot hold two tigers. The apparently coordinated onslaught was a terrifying mystery to the villagers who remained baffled by it years later. The tigers held their ground for three days, trapping the inhabitants. Some speculated that there was a "Tiger King" that led the band of marauders. After three days the big cats stormed the village in a coordinated attack and ransacked the livestock. The humans froze, petrified, locked in their houses, except for one little girl who wandered out at the wrong moment and was snatched up by a huge beast.

The incident may not perhaps be completely unique. As we saw earlier, a report in 1936 from Guangdong province told of a daily tiger siege at a village of some 60 people. It did not go into the numbers, but a group of tigers were making daily raids that the villagers were helpless to defend themselves from. They resorted to barring their doors and locking themselves in every afternoon from one to five, the so-called "feeding time" of the big cats.

Nevertheless, tiger sieges are rare according to the available literature, and the 1957 drama that ended in a violent explosion appeared to be one of the last acts of defiance from a dying population, a subspecies on its way to extinction. The anti-tiger movement had followed the national policy of "Bending Nature to the Will of the People" by sending teams of peasants and soldiers out to encircle tigers in their lairs and use guns and grenades on their targets, and it worked only too well.

By the end of the 1950s the hunt was getting harder because the numbers were dwindling. Once the residual populations had reduced to small hidden pockets, the heavy weapons of modern warfare were no longer efficient. Traditional crossbow traps became more suitable, as something that could be set up and left in place, allowing the hunter to sit and wait instead of going on an impossible search for a lone cat in the vast and emptied wilderness.

After 1963 there were no more tiger injuries reported in Hunan, and by the following year the last tiger team there was disbanded. There was little left to do. Other than occasional sightings for another decade or so, the South China tiger had all but disappeared in that province, while exactly the same thing was happening in the rest of its territory, including Guangdong province, Hong Kong's old home and future destiny once Britain's lease would expire.

Right royal tiger slaughter

Until very recently, millions of humans have coexisted close to tigers. From the Caspian Sea in the west, to the eastern edge of the Asian landmass in the Korean peninsula, and from the northern chill of Siberia down through the sweltering Sundarbans and way further south as far as the beautiful island of Bali, the tiger lived cheek-by-jowl with people well into the 20th century. Local knowledge and years of sound advice passed down through generations fabricated a balance in places, where humans and tigers gave each the space and respect needed for an uneasy but somehow manageable truce.

But just as often, the peace would crumble and man and beast resumed their war.

A fascinating question would be to ask if we have even co-evolved with these adversaries. Have our senses, instincts and intellect been sharpened by the tiger? Has the tiger's intelligence developed at least in part in reaction to our own scheming cunning? We don't know the answer to these big questions, but what we do know is that where the uneasy balance between humans and big cats has toppled off-kilter, the tiger can turn on us with the mighty wrath of a vengeful deranged deity. As an opportunist it is an efficient killer, swiping a lone grass-cutter here, grabbing a child there. Sometimes it is much more than that. It becomes a systematic hunter of people, a "man-eater", regaining its title as the apex predator.

Records show that tens of thousands of humans have been killed by tigers around the world, including thousands in China in the 20th century. In southern China, Harry Caldwell documented in detail the devastating effect that rogue tigers were having on some communities. Lives were snuffed out, villages torn apart. Terrified survivors were stricken by paralysis. Crops went untended and whole regions could fall into poverty when a handful of big cats went on the prowl.

It might be tempting to look back and imagine some visionary taking grip of the situation in China in the 1950s, setting up sanctuaries and preserving the fantastic beasts in pristine, protected forests. All the while peasant farmers could have tapped into their ancestral memories to remember how to live in peace with the awesome mammals, reaching back through millennia of folklore and wisdom.

But that is not what happened, and let's not forget that many of the problem beasts were not really living in the wilderness. They were scavenging on the edge of human settlements, eating dogs and pigs, their owners, and their owners' children.

Considering all that, it is fair to say that something needed to be done in the highly populated southern Chinese provinces in the mid-20th century. Whether the right thing was done, or if it was done in the right way, is a matter for debate that can and should take place. But it is hard to argue that there wasn't some necessity for action, and we should not be too quick to judge the Chinese anti-tiger campaigns of the 1950s, as devastating as they were.

Aristocrats travelling to foreign lands to sit on the backs of elephants, shooting wildlife for fun, however, look like a different proposition altogether. Did British royals for example need to go to India and Nepal to kill wildlife in the 1960s?

Newspaper reports from the time say that Queen Elizabeth's husband Philip shot a tiger in India in 1961, at a time that was the brink of catastrophe for large carnivorous wildlife populations. The royal couple were on a five-week goodwill tour of the Commonwealth, and India was the first stop. Buckingham Palace had publicised in advance the news that the Maharaja of Jaipur had invited the couple to a tiger shoot.

"Prince Philip might be expected to take a fairly active role but it will be up to the Queen to decide how active a part she will play, depending on how she feels," a palace spokesperson said in a statement that by today's standards sounds a tad tone-deaf.

The Duke of Edinburgh didn't disappoint his hosts. "Prince Philip has shot his tiger. Not face to face. In fact, the Prince shot the tiger from a platform up a tree," a scandalised *Daily Mirror* raged on a front-page editorial. "It happened yesterday in India in the Rajasthan jungle near Jaipur."

"But is there anything to be pleased about in this unhappy episode? Or does it illustrate again the huge gap between the hunting and shooting habits of the Royal Family and feelings of the British public towards animals?" the paper asked. Hong Kong's *China Mail*, which was reporting on the *Mirror*'s editorial, made sure readers in the crown colony, who might have been unaware of the politics of the homeland's tabloids, understood that the *Mirror* was a left-wing newspaper.

We are often told that we shouldn't judge the actions of people in the past with the standards of today, but just as often it is forgotten that there were plenty of social critics at the time who made public their dissent. It isn't so much that the ideas have changed, it's the relative popularity of ideas that change with fashion.

Not to be outdone by India, Nepal laid on a huge hunting expedition for the royal couple on the same tour a few weeks later. "King Mahendra, one of the world's 15 best shots, will give the honour of the first shot to the Duke of Edinburgh – and Nepalis said their tiny nation will be disappointed unless the Duke kills at least three tigers," a correspondent reported in the *China Mail* on 21st February 1961. The couple were invited to the Chitwan valley, to a specially constructed four square mile hunting village of luxury tents with private bathrooms and hot running water. The area was covered in DDT to kill off unwanted insects, and all the turf dug up and relaid having been cleared of jungle bugs. Three hundred soldiers, beaters and elephant boys, with three hundred elephants, were on hand. The Nepalis were hoping the Queen would be tempted to take a shot herself.

It was the ultimate staged hunt. The area was prepared for weeks in advance by baiting tigers with fat buffaloes enough times to make the tigers used to come looking for their free handouts. On the day of the hunt the elephant handlers formed a ring around the area and moved inwards to close the circle. Beaters in front of the elephants also stretched white cloth between them in the belief that tigers were afraid of the flapping white sheets and could not jump over them to escape the shrinking circle. Eventually the wildlife would be forced into a cleared shooting ground, where royals could pick them off easily from the backs of elephants. The Nepalis said this would be the biggest and most spectacular shoot since the Queen's grandfather, King George V, shot from a 600-elephant ring in 1911. It was a far cry from a professional hunter patiently tracking a known man-eating prowler.

As if all that wasn't enough, the Nepalis were planning to give the Queen a feast during her stay at the camp, including a serving of a species of crane that was known then to be almost extinct.

Mahendra ruled Nepal until 1972 when he was succeeded by his son Birendra, whose reign ended in 2001 in a bloody massacre. He was murdered, along with eight other members of the royal household, by his son Crown Prince Dipendra. The murderer saved his last shot for himself, but failed in his bid for a quick death, and fell into a coma. Thus Mahendra's grandson was declared king after unleashing a brutal killing spree, though his reign only lasted three days in a coma until his life was finally snuffed out. The royal lineage limped on for another six years until Maoists forced the abolition of the 239-year-old Nepalese monarchy in 2007. Today there are more than 230 tigers in Nepal, according to Nepal's National Trust for Nature Conservation, formerly named the King Mahendra Trust for Nature Conservation, with environmentalists expressing cautious hope that the Nepalese tiger may have been saved by recent conservation efforts. The big cats predated the monarchy that hunted them for sport, and they have outlasted them.

The Shing Mun rambler

Considering the timeline of the Chinese campaign against tigers, and the generally precarious times for the world's big mammals, it seems remarkable that there is one more notable tiger episode in Hong Kong that was convincing enough for police and Gurkha soldiers to set out hunting.

It was 1965, three years after Typhoon Wanda had ploughed into Hong Kong leaving 130 people dead, 53 missing, more than 2,000 small craft wrecked, sunk or damaged, and 36 ocean-going vessels floundering. The Vietnam War was already raging, with the United States taking off its cloak of invisibility in Southeast Asia and openly shipping troops to battle. That was part of a chain of events which would later help to flush a new wave of refugees towards the colony. 1965 was also one year after Britain's globe-conquering pop band, The Beatles, came to town on a completely different type of cultural revolution from the one that Mao would kick-start shortly in the mainland. The world was already unrecognisable from the one where shirtless and emaciated Hong Kong officials had shuffled out of the barbed-wire enclosure of Stanley internment camp just 20 years earlier.

Biologist Dr Malcolm Peaker recently recalled the atmosphere surrounding the Shing Mun Valley tiger. He had arrived in Hong Kong for a post at the university's zoology department a few months after the reports had trickled out so he missed the immediate excitement. "There was talk in the zoology department that this could have been a genuine case," he wrote.

It started with a 19-year-old school girl, So Ka-ling, a pupil of the Diocesan Girls' School, who was on an outing with friends near the Shing Mun Reservoir, also known as the Jubilee Reservoir. She said she saw an animal that was about three or four feet high, decorated with black and white stripes.

It was enough to set off the first of many searches over several weeks by the authorities, who took the report seriously. Inspector Luk Hung-kuen led seven hunters and five reporters to the west side of Tai Mo Shan on an exhausting and fruitless trek through thorny trails and rocky stream beds. The official party was not the only one on the hunt. They came across a lone hunter armed only with two bamboo poles and a portable radio, who had also heard about So Ka-ling's encounter. He explained to reporters that his radio was for music "to give me courage when I meet the tiger", before he disappeared into obscurity.

A few days later Wong Kwok, a Kowloon Motor Bus driver from Yuen Long, spotted the Shing Mun rambler and took a shot. The thought of gun-toting bus drivers in the Hong Kong of the swinging sixties is intriguing, but Wong was no crack shot by his own account. He couldn't say if he had hit the feline, but now there was the worry that an injured tiger may well be on the prowl. Police followed up and found six "very clear" pug marks approximately seven inches across. A determined Wong kept an all-night vigil in the hope of following up with the definitive shot, but still had no success.

A couple of days later more paw marks were found on the north side of the reservoir. These were confirmed by Yip Yun-shiu, an Agricultural and Forestry Department worker. A professor of the zoology department at the University of Hong Kong told the *South China Morning Post* that the spoors were consistent with a 300-pound tiger.

Some 200 labourers on the Shing Mun Reservoir were ordered to stop work to make way for an army tiger hunt. Major G.G. Roach led a team of Gurkhas in an operation that started with the construction of tree-top observation platforms that supported marksmen armed with automatic weapons. Live goats were brought in as bait near the watch posts that were manned through the night by four Gurkhas from the 67 Independent Field Squadron, and two from the 2nd Battalion 7th Duke of Edinburgh's Own Gurkha Rifles.

It yielded nothing.

Five days later there were several reports of growls, a few miles away to the northwest and over the other side of Tai Mo Shan at Pat Heung. A group of police officers were among those who heard roars, including Inspector Chik of the Pat Heung Police Station. Another officer in the party was from Pakistan and had game hunting experience. He confirmed the sounds were consistent with a hungry but aged big cat. Tang Koon-fat, one of the three watchmen hired by the army, also heard growls from about 200 yards away. Villagers from Ta Shek Wu added their reports. Farmer Tse Ching-chi heard three roars, a pause and another roar. Village dogs were in a frenzy.

Inspector Chik placed his men in a semi-circle to protect the village. He noted that the growls came at intervals and stopped when cars passed. They used police Land Rovers to light up the area, but they did not get a sighting. The top of the hill was unguarded. The party stayed in place until five in the morning and returned the following afternoon with Gurkhas to comb the area. They still had no luck, though they were sufficiently concerned to make the village a no-go area for outsiders not involved in the hunt.

Despite the various signs of the tiger that had been recorded for a number of days, the *SCMP* received an anonymous call claiming the whole affair was a hoax. The caller said that the footprints had been faked using a stuffed tiger paw. Dr Ian Thornton of the Hong Kong University zoology department said the photos he had been shown by the police looked genuine, though he also said it would be impossible to tell if a stuffed paw was used just from looking at the photos. Weighing it up he concluded "there is some evidence that there is a tiger in the New Territories." The police were also nonplussed about the fake claims. A senior officer told the *SCMP* that they "are still treating the report of the tiger as genuine. Until there is evidence to prove that the tiger is made of paper then the search will continue."

The following day, on 5th August, officials called off that particular search, but more would follow. Police kept the area of the sightings closed and advised all picnickers and sightseers to stay away even as a new report of a sighting in Yuen Long suggested the surveillance area should be broadened. Determined amateurs put together their own plans, such as a scheme to set up a network of 100 tethered goats over the New Territories, fitted with microphones or bells to capture data on the whereabouts of the Shing Mun rambler. The information would be relayed through a network of walkie-talkie-carrying volunteers.

The reports continued throughout August. Hunts, official and amateur, were called, called off, called again. Buffaloes were tied up as bait, pigs went missing. Lai Tong Kwok, headmaster of the Tai Mei Tuk primary school, heard growls on a Sunday evening. A special 10-man police group who attended lectures on the habits of tigers and trained in range shooting were on standby to follow up on reports. Mr Yip Loy spotted the animal on a Friday morning on a hillside opposite Siu Lo Poon village, and two Chinese ladies saw it over at Plover Cove, triggering a 40-man search in the area.

But excitement was fading.

In September a construction worker saw 10.5-inch paw prints in the playground of Chung Chi College, in the sandy earth on the race track. He had heard growls the night before as he slept on a construction site nearby, and this is the last trace of the Shing Mun rambler which left us so many clues, but no conclusive proof that it had been here.

More than 20 years later, Chief Superintendent Gwyn Lloyd of the Hong Kong police, who had been a young inspector in 1965, told the *South China Morning Post:* "In my mind there was something. The witnesses had no reason to lie. As for the villagers, these were basic down-to-earth country folk who wanted nothing to do with authority and had never done so, yet they still called us. If you go on these facts it seems reasonable."

The ghost of the South China tiger
After September 1965, tiger reports in Hong Kong dropped off dramatically. For those paying attention, such accounts had been a regular occurrence throughout the 20th century, interrupted only by war, and slowing down only in the 10 years leading up to the Shing Mun rambler. But that year marks a turning point, after which tiger reports become rare, more doubtful, and much less substantial.

The wild population had plummeted. Some 1,000 tigers were estimated to remain in southern China by 1965, as the mainland government kept tabs on pelts being sold. The first five years of that decade saw an average of 125 skins per year registered for export, while the corresponding period of the previous decade saw some 400 entering the market each year.

No doubt unaware of the extent of the tiger population collapse in the mainland, farmers in Hong Kong were gripped by fear following the mysterious death of a cow in 1971. Villagers of Shatin, many of whom remembered tiger attacks in previous decades, said the cow's left ear, tail and part of the rump were bitten off, though at least one vet had a very different view. He said the animal had died during a miscarriage.

In a sign of changing sensibilities, the reporter noted that Mrs Law Tai-kiu had lost her only cow and would now be plunged into a life of uncertainty. "It was my only means to farm paddy fields to earn my living. It was my whole property," she said. In older reports, the question of the well-being of the people who lost cattle or pigs was seldom given any attention.

Five years later, at the end of China's disastrous Cultural Revolution, a Lok Ma Chau villager, right on the border with the mainland, told police of a tiger seen twice in ten days, roaming about after dark. The *SCMP* reported this on 12th September, 1976, just three days after the death of Mao Zedong. Some Chinese traditions state that the sighting of a tiger spelled a regime change. The villager said the animal was about three feet high, four feet long and dark. Police found pug marks and the case was handed over to the Agriculture and Fisheries Department for further investigation. Two years later China's new leader, Deng Xiaoping, would be in the area, laying the foundations of what would become the mega-city of Shenzhen, almost sealing nature's corridor between the mainland and Hong Kong, though to this day that proposition has never been completed and a large artery of greenery remains on the eastern side of the border.

If these South China tiger sightings were not mistaken they were surely among the last glimpses of what at that time was probably the rarest tiger subspecies in the world. The mainland's export markets still legally traded skins, but only one or two a year were being registered in the early 1970s. Concerned biologists realised something had gone terribly wrong. With the wild population plunging to its last 30 or 40 by the 1980s, the subspecies was on an irreversible spiral towards extinction.

In Hong Kong, as British Prime Minister Margaret Thatcher had started negotiations with Deng Xiaoping on Britain's final withdrawal from a borrowed land, officials were taking plaster cast prints of a suspected tiger near Tai Lam Chung reservoir. Villagers at Tin Fu had reported loud roars and the Agriculture and Fisheries Department turned to big game hunters for their guns and skills. It was 15 years before London's 99-year lease on the New Territories was to expire, perhaps the last paw print of a tiger in Hong Kong, and perhaps the last on the last scrap of Victoria's once mighty empire.

In the following decade scientists went on a desperate search through southern China, sometimes with local guides who had intimate knowledge that was gained from their own hunting days when all they wanted was to lob a grenade at a thieving scavenger. The Chinese development dream was coming to fruition, and wealth had flowed inland from the coastline. Soon the country would boast the most billionaires of any nation except the United States. Thus with one of the Communist Party's revised developmental goals nearly achieved, all was forgiven with the tiger. The revered big cats could have some space after all. In fact surely the Lord of the Hundred Beasts rightfully belonged in a country of proud and patriotic socialist billionaires.

The only problem was that they weren't there any more.

There were signs, tracks and scrapes, reports of roars that rumbled through to the end of the millennium. The last officially confirmed sighting was in the early 1970s, though one elderly hunter told Chris Coggins that he had killed his last tiger in 1982. A few remaining wanderers left their calling cards on tree trunks that they gouged with deep grooves. These scrapes and their tracks were seen into the 1990s in reserves in Fujian, Hunan and Guangdong. But the tiger, a master illusionist at the best of times, turned into a ghost, a haunting from a lost world that had existed for hundreds of thousands of years before disappearing – just yesterday, it seems. Camera trap surveys of the past 20 years have not yielded a single fragment of striped anatomy, not a leg, not an ear, not even a tail end.

With the wild population functionally extinct, the Chinese government has set up schemes to bring some back to life in protected reserves. In the early 2000s, authorities identified 57 genuine South China tigers in captivity and assigned their genes to the effort for the resurrection of *panthera tigris amoyensis*. Every animal born in this programme will be logged, supervised and supported. Every detail of their lives will be managed from birth to death and beyond. Not everyone will recognise these animals to be the wild beasts that wandered in and out of Hong Kong on a regular basis until well into the 1950s and possibly the 1960s. Those huge predators snuck around all over southern China, undermined and unravelled human authority, brought chaos at will, destroyed property, and killed, before disappearing into the night.

In Hong Kong, as in China, and all over the planet, the hairless monkey is an enigma. We are vicious, vengeful and ruthlessly destructive. We have willingly exterminated whole species. We reserve our worst cruelties for ourselves. At the same time we are sentimental, remorseful and even self-sacrificing. We desperately care, we love and we have hope. We want the tigers back, though not necessarily in our own backyard.

Any tigers watching us would easily conclude that humans are mad, bonkers, stark raving lunatics.

So the dream lives on, even if the tiger didn't.

Chapter 10

CHASING THE HONG KONG TIGER

Today

The missing cats

In my first few years of living in Hong Kong I believed that there were two tiger stories relating to the city. The first was the 1915 Sheung Shui tiger and the second was the 1942 Stanley tiger. Automatically I had made an assumption that those were the last two of an indigenous population, the last tigers of Hong Kong. Thinking back, I find it strange, and embarrassing that I saw no need to question such a proposal, even as I got to know the local wildlife better and developed an appreciation for the biodiversity, the rich environment and dramatic landscape of the place. The question took a long time to emerge: were those two really the last tigers of the territory?

I remember the moment clearly.

I was reading an article about tigers by Jonathan Downes in *Porcupine*, the newsletter of the Hong Kong University Department of Ecology and Biodiversity. In a discussion on the tiny population of South China tigers that remained in the wild by the 1990s, he pointed out that "well within living memory, however [the tigers were] far more widespread, and there have been many well documented accounts of visits by tigers to Hong Kong." It was a penny-dropping moment for me and the key word was "visit".

The fate of Hong Kong tigers was not separate from the fate of China's tigers. Once you stop thinking about an indigenous population, and you start to appreciate that Hong Kong is simply one part of an ecosystem much larger than the territory itself, it becomes clear that each tiger spotted in the territory was the sighting of an interloper. While there was an abundance of them in the region, their appearance in Hong Kong from time to time was to be expected. This is not a difficult concept for anyone who has come to appreciate the thousands of migratory birds that arrive each year from the Arctic circle, Central Asian plains or anywhere on the vast Austral-Asian flyway. Yet for some reason we don't apply that thought too much to large carnivorous mammals.

Downes went on to cite the clear and unambiguous words of Geoffrey Herklots, calling him "the greatest single naturalist" ever to work in Hong Kong: "nearly every winter one or more tigers visit the New Territories."

As exciting as it was, it took a while to get beyond that breakthrough.

Of course there must have been more tigers than the 1915 and the 1942 celebrities, but where were they? I went in search for natural history books and journals to find evidence, and I spoke to experts who knew the region, and enthusiasts with knowledge and appreciation of Hong Kong's wildlife and history. No one I spoke to had any information about the missing tigers, and very little appeared in print.

One constant in print and among experts was a universal respect for Herklots. I had first come across his work in *Hong Kong Naturalist* articles archived online by the University of Hong Kong. There we had some of the tiger gaps filled, with vivid descriptions of apparitions in the 1930s. As fascinating as they were, they only amounted to about five or six different tigers. Of course Herklots had an interest in them, but he had an interest in every living organism of the colony. There were only so many tiger stories that could be accommodated. These were collected in the short tiger section of his 1951 book *The Hong Kong Countryside*.

Other than that I found virtually nothing about Hong Kong's missing tigers. Online searches mostly brought up articles that faithfully and always briefly recounted the 1915 and the 1942 tigers, though there were a handful of reports that referred to Herklots' other 1930s tigers, and some references to the 1965 tiger hunts.

C.T. Shek's *A Field Guide to the Terrestrial Mammals of Hong Kong* makes a tiny reference to tigers, citing Herklots again to state that according to his records the South China tiger and the leopard were regular winter visitors, adding no more details. In *A Colour Guide to Hong Kong Animals* by Hill and Phillipps, published in 1981, we learn simply that "The last recorded tiger was shot in the New Territories in 1915".

I got in touch with Dr Gary Ades of Kadoorie Farm. He told me that the wide green corridor that linked Hong Kong with Shenzhen would have allowed tigers to roam freely in search of wild boar and barking deer. He also said that in lean times, hunger would drive them closer to livestock and human settlements. Other than that he did not have information about actual sightings within Hong Kong.

I contacted Dr Malcolm Peaker, a biologist who had taught at Hong Kong University in the 1960s. He had just arrived in the city after the 1965 tiger reports, he told me. So he had missed the excitement and the chase for the evidence, but he did recall that the general belief in the department was that it had been a genuine case. I asked if the department might have kept notes by Herklots from an earlier age and he told me all the pre-1940s documents had been destroyed in the Japanese occupation. Hong Kong's missing tigers remained elusive.

I found the works of Chris Coggins online and bought his book *The Tiger and the Pangolin* to learn about the South China tiger. I called him and he explained how he studied the "longest written chronological account of human wildlife interactions in the world" to discover how the South China tiger had prowled the four provinces of Fujian, Jiangxi, Hunan and Guangdong for centuries, leaving a 1,900-year record of encounters with humans. He had met surviving members of the mainland's 1950s pest extermination campaigns, and had gone to the mountains with them to search for signs of remnant tiger life in the 1990s. And though he had described documents that recalled tigers in Guangdong's Pearl River delta, his main focus was on the tiger heartlands in Fujian and he had very little to say about the appearances of the tiger inside the borders of Hong Kong. In conversation with me he accepted the proposal of tigers turning up in the territory as perfectly plausible, but it simply wasn't an area he had looked into.

Coggins gave me other contacts to follow up, South China tiger experts who would be happy to talk with me. A consistent pattern emerged. People who knew about the South China tiger generally found it interesting to consider the proposition that the species occasionally wandered over the border into the British crown colony, but they themselves had little information to add to the story. After all, Hong Kong wasn't the place researchers headed to if they set out to study tigers.

I went looking for sources at the Central Library in Causeway Bay. There were tiger books and there were China books, and then there were Hong Kong books. You can learn about carnivorous felines in China, or you can read books about the history or natural history or ecology of Hong Kong. You can even read books that place Hong Kong within the southern China ecosystem, but you can't find books specifically about tigers in Hong Kong. You can discover Hong Kong's civet cats and macaques, you can even educate yourself on leopard cats in the territory. But there was nothing bringing the two ends of my particular thread together.

I sat down at a computer assigned to the Multimedia Information System of the Hong Kong Public Libraries. It offered a search of archived newspapers going back more than a hundred years. I typed in the word "tiger" and clicked through the early decades of the 20th century. Blotchy digitised 100-year-old print started appearing. The simple search had revealed a stream of tiger stories from the region. There were Indian and Malayan man-eaters, tiger battles in Java, villages under siege in China, hunters on the prowl.

Then, at last, I started finding the Hong Kong stories.

An unfinished story

The first decade of the 1900s was sketchy and there were more reports from mainland trading posts than there were from Hong Kong itself. The picture they painted of the local tiger scene was as blotchy as the digitised print. Dead cows, the occasional pig disappearance, unconfirmed sightings, a person mauled. Intriguing mysteries that faded to obscurity and offered little in the way of evidence, except collectively when seen for their consistency and frequency, in a pattern that reaches into the second half of the century.

There was sarcasm and scorn in many of the local reports, a tone that would never be shaken off despite years of similar stories laying down layers of consistent evidence that tigers kept returning and returning until their population collapsed in the mainland. The pendulum could swing sometimes when there were "impeccable" witnesses and "trustworthy" sources, and belief in tigers was accepted briefly as if respectable society had never doubted it in the first place, only to collapse again quickly in a heap of uncertainty.

But as we entered the second decade of Britain's hold over the New Territories, the stories of tigers mounted until the key moment at Sheung Shui mid-decade that proved once and for all that tigers in Hong Kong were a fact of life, and death.

There they were, the territory's missing tigers, as Herklots had suggested they would be, in print, in black and white. The papers corroborated the accepted incidents – the famed felines of 1915 and 1942. And they backed up the handful Herklots had recorded in the 1930s. They filled in the background of the 1965 apparition with a series of detailed reports in the *SCMP*, and having ticked those cross-checking points, they filled in the big gaps in between, with tigers spotted here, there and everywhere, most years, many times over in the first five decades of the 1900s. The Hong Kong countryside was strewn with carcasses of domestic cattle and swine torn apart by the wild predator. Hong Kong's missing tigers were jumping out of preserved newsprint well into the mid-20th century.

What became obvious was that there had to be people alive today who could tell me personally about the tigers of Hong Kong. Having found the evidence in print, I went in search of the keepers of the collective memory.

I had early successes with two of my friends who had parents with personal stories of big cats from their years of growing up in the New Territories. But overall the results were frustrating and I believe were limited by the fact that my family and I had come to the end of our stay in Hong Kong. After spending 20 years of my life in southern China's much-storied city, I had to pack my bags and get back to the UK. Collected below are the results of my pursuit of the personal stories. I preserve them here with some contextual information to show some of the process of chasing up these memories, and what kind of barriers there are in extracting them, including my Japanese surname!

I remain convinced that there are many more Hong Kong tiger tales out there, even as the clock is ticking on the generation that would have personal experience of the King of Cats inside the boundaries of the city. For that reason I would like to appeal to anyone who has got as far as this point in the book, who has any leads on this, to get in touch via my publisher at *www.blacksmithbooks.com* because I am convinced that this work is far from finished.

John Saeki
February 2022

Grandma's tiger

Hi John,

Finally got round to asking my mum about tigers! Here goes:

My mum was born in 1938 and grew up in Ting Kok village which is in the Tai Po area. It's overlooked by the Pat Sin Leng mountain range. They lived a very rural life and went up and down the Pat Sin Leng mountains for firewood, which they carried into town and sold or exchanged for food.

She never saw a tiger herself. However, my grandma did one time when she went up Pat Sin Leng to cut firewood. They stuck to the same area which was about 30 minutes hike uphill from the village. My mum believes she was between 12 and 14 years old at the time so it would have been around 1950-1952. My grandma had said the tiger wasn't particularly big. She had been terrified and so had run back down to the village.

Around that time, the tiger had also eaten a cow and a pig from Ting Kok village. My mum knows the daughter of the family who lost the cow. That family took their cattle up the mountains to graze each morning and they made their way back to the village at dusk. One day, one of the smaller cows didn't return. My mum went along with a small search party to look for it. They carried lanterns and loud gongs to make noise to scare away the tiger. They eventually found the remains of the cow and my mum said there had been an official examination of the carcass which confirmed a tiger attack. The pig was taken from its sty in the village. The villagers had heard the pig squealing as it was carried away in the direction of the mountain. Also, she recalled another lady had seen a tiger sleeping one day when she was in the mountains.

Everyone was wary that there was a tiger in that mountain area at the time with the attacks and sightings. My mum was scared going up and down there for firewood. Her great-grandma had taught her that if she saw a tiger, she should run downhill rather than up (she'd been told tigers were slow and clumsy descenders as they had shorter front legs) and to run diagonally rather than straight. Also, she'd been taught that birds go quiet in the presence of tigers and so if everything was silent in the mountains, then that could be because a tiger was nearby.

My mum recalled that some Westerners from Hong Kong Island started to go shooting in the Pat Sin Leng area at some point in the 1950s. They came at weekends with dogs and rifles. The tiger sightings and attacks stopped at some point after that.

She thinks the shooting scared them off (they were shooting for birds).

I also asked if she remembered any tiger sightings or attacks in my dad's village, which is Lin Au. She said she didn't. She'd moved to that village in the late 1950s.

Hope this helps.

Ann

Dead cow falling

Me: Hi Mike, do you recall any tiger stories in your family as you were growing up?

Mike: Tigers? I don't think so. My dad did used to talk about lions though.

Me: Wow! Lions. I haven't heard about them in Hong Kong, but I would love to hear about it if he can recall.

Mike: Let me check with him, he lives in England now.

. . .

Mike: Hi John, I spoke to my dad. You were right, it was a tiger, not a lion! I got the Chinese character mixed up.

Me: Ah, I thought so.

Mike: He remembers villagers talking about tigers when he was growing up. He didn't see one himself, but he did see a dead cow falling off a mountain. It had been attacked by a tiger.

Me: Wow. Do you think he would be willing to talk to me about that?

Mike: Let me check.

. . .

Mike: Hi John, my dad's going to be back in Hong Kong in a few weeks.

Me: Great!

Mike: I can take you up to our village where he would be happy to talk about tigers.

Me: Fantastic.

Mike: I'll get back to you when he has made his plans.

. . .

Mike: Hi John, I've been speaking to the parents and at this stage they are really not keen on coming to HK right now because of the protests and they are taking a wait and see approach. Will keep you posted and in the meantime I hope you are making progress on the research!

Me: Oh, sure, I completely understand.

Face to face with a very large cat

Dear John,

My father took his family at every available hour into the Hong Kong hills, usually along with his great friend the botanist Geoffrey Herklots. On this occasion we were to call in for tea on an elderly Dutch couple who lived on a remote headland overlooking Starling Cove.

I think it was in 1948, I was six years old and exploring ahead of the main group. I remember trotting round a bend in the path and coming face to face with this very large cat. Our eyes were on the same level! I think we were both as startled as each other. I was paralysed partly with shock and partly fascination!

The huge cat was the first to move and sloped off into the undergrowth. I came to, and raced back to the rest of the party babbling about my experience; I wasn't taken seriously, thinking that I was either exaggerating or making it all up.

A couple of days later there was a report in the *South China Morning Post* of villagers' chickens stolen by a tiger.

Maybe the big cat was full of those villagers' chickens and wasn't the least bit hungry when we met!

Best wishes from Veronica

A pair of tigers at dusk

Kai: Dear John,
A reply from the NGO. Looks exciting.

Mr. Cheung grew up in Sha Lo Tung, Tai Po, N.T., Hong Kong. He was born in 1932.
He saw a pair of tigers walking towards him from the gap to Ping Shan Tsai near Sha Lo Tung. It was dusk, one or two years after the end of WWII. He saw their outlines clearly. Afterwards, he saw the footprints of tigers many times in Sha Lo Tung.
Mr. Cheung heard his uncle's grandpa had shot at a tiger. The tiger was grasping a pig beside the stream in Cheung Uk. It fled when the shot was fired.
Mr. Cheung's mother also saw tigers.
Mr. Cheung recalled an expatriate hunter who was injured by a tiger. He was part of a team that came looking for tigers near Sha Lo Tung and had been guided by locals.

. . .

Me: Hi Kai, this is great. Do you think there could be any chance of me interviewing him? Although I am sorry to say I don't speak Cantonese.

. . .

Kai: Hi John, sorry to tell you that Mr Cheng, who took down Mr Cheung's account, was hoping to avoid this type of meeting. As you are Japanese, and Mr Cheung suffered badly during the Japanese occupation, Mr Cheng thought it better you didn't meet up. I hope you understand the difficulty.

. . .

Me: Hi there Kai, thank you for your kind efforts. I appreciate your emails and all these follow up details. It is unfortunate about him not wanting to speak to a Japanese but I totally understand, considering what happened during the occupation. Please let Mr Cheng and Mr Cheung know that I am grateful for all they have told me already.

Tiger on Lazy Man's Rock

Amy/Luke: If this is the correct email address, I may have a contact for you from an 86-year-old woman who lived in the Ma On Shan mountain area. She has a tiger story from the 1950s, I think.
Please respond and I'll ask if she's willing to speak with you. She speaks little/no English.

Me: Hi there, indeed this is the right email for tiger stories. Thank you very much for getting in contact. I would love to hear this lady's story.

. . .

Amy/Luke: Hi John,
We sat with Mrs Cheung on International Women's Day to discuss your questions. I am sending you the recordings. We hope that Mrs Cheung has been of assistance to you.

. . .

Me: Hi Pete, How are you doing? Been crazy here, as I'm sure it is everywhere. Someone has kindly interviewed a lively elderly lady talking about her tiger-kill experience. She sounds very animated and fascinating. Do you think you could help me get a transcription? It could just complete the book.
Pete: Hi John, translations are in train, and I'll send them back to you asap.

. . .

Taken from audio recordings with Mrs (Granny) Cheung:

I was born in Wong Chuk Yeung, Sai Kung, in 1933. Villagers there farmed and repaired things.

There were twenty-five or twenty-six families, and a lot of farms there, where people usually grew vegetables. I grew up in that village.

I was fifteen or sixteen when I heard about tigers around. People were scared that their cows would be eaten. Tigers love to eat cows.

I didn't see any tigers eating cows, but later on they were there, in another village.

There were many tigers in Shap Sze Heung near Sha Tin.

Those days, people would close their gates by six or seven in the evening because they were afraid tigers would eat their cows.

There was a wild boar that fought with a tiger on the farm where my mom and many other farmers worked. The boar had come to eat the crops in the field that were nearly ready for harvesting. The tiger was really big and it was very clever. It didn't eat the boar in the field, but it dragged it away to the mountainside, leaving a trail of blood along the route. Men from the village found the carcass when they got up to irrigate the fields. The remains of the boar were covered in leaves. Of course they knew the boar had been eaten by the tiger. If not, who would eat it? In those days the boars liked to eat the crops that were mature and about to be harvested. It was devastating to have the yields gone like this.

The tiger had dragged the boar a long way. Villagers walked 15 minutes along the blooded route to find the boar remains. They brought the carcass back. Only two legs had been eaten by the tiger and there was much of the body left, which was then divided by the village people.

My mom ate some, but I didn't.

I only saw the dead boar, but not the tiger.

Also there was an uncle in the village who saw a tiger in the field another time.

When he went to check how much water was left in the field, he saw a white tiger sitting there, holding its tongue out, as it probably smelled the cows and wanted to eat them. He was ten or twenty years older than me, married with kids. He ran away when he saw the tiger. His face turned white with fear when he got back, crying and shouting "Aiya, there's a tiger sitting on the Lazy Man's Rock!"

People said, "Oh, the cows would be eaten by it then."

His face turned white with fear when he got back, crying and shouting "Aiya, there's a tiger sitting on the Lazy Man's Rock!"

It was around 9 o'clock, and the cows were set free at the field. Every night if they hadn't returned, villagers had to go out to look for them in the mountain.

I was among those back in the village who heard about the tiger in the field.

But the tiger must have gone without killing any cows. Tigers are clever, they don't want to be beaten by villagers.

They said that tigers were coming from mainland China, some even swam over here.

I don't want to talk too much about tigers.

. . .

Luke: Hi John, we spoke to Mrs Cheung yesterday. She accepts your thanks.
There do appear to be more stories in the villages running along Ma On Shan. The first-hand stories are from those in their mid-80s and above that age. The second-hand stories are from those who spoke to people now gone who might still serve as a story reservoir.
Me: Thanks Luke. I'm pretty sure there are many more stories out there.

BIBLIOGRAPHY

Sources of tiger stories
China Mail
Hong Kong Telegraph
South China Morning Post (SCMP)
Hong Kong Daily Press
Hong Kong Sunday Telegraph
Hong Kong Sunday Herald
Hong Kong Naturalist

Hong Kong's environment and ecology
Hong Kong University Biology Department – *Hong Kong Naturalist* journal, 1930-41
G.A.C. Herklots – *The Hong Kong Countryside Throughout the Seasons*
Dennis S. Hill, Karen Phillipps – *A Colour Guide to Hong Kong Animals*
C.T. Shek – *A Field Guide to the Terrestrial Mammals of Hong Kong*
John Strickland – *Southern District Officer Reports: Islands and Villages in Rural Hong Kong*
Porcupine: HKU ecology and biodiversity – https://porcupinehku. wordpress.com/about
Malcolm Peaker – https://zoologyweblog.blogspot.com

China's environment and ecology
Harry R. Caldwell – *Blue Tiger*
Chris Coggins – *The Tiger and the Pangolin: Nature, culture, and conservation in China*

John Caldwell – *China Coast Family*
Kathy Traylor-Holzer, Ronald Tilson, Qui Ming Jiang – *The decline and impending extinction of the South China tiger*, 1997 article
Nicki Chen – http://nickichenwrites.com/wordpress

Tiger facts, nature, zoology and environment
John Vaillant – *The Tiger*
David Prynn – *Amur Tiger*
George M. Eberhar – *Mysterious Creatures: A Guide to Cryptozoology, Volume 2*
Ronald Tilson, Philip J. Nyhus – *Tigers of the World: The Science, Politics and Conservation of Panthera tigris*
Gordon Grice – *The Book of Deadly Animals*
Sea World Parks – https://seaworld.org/animals/all-about/tiger/characteristics

History
Frank Welsh – *A History of Hong Kong*
Geoffrey Charles Emerson – *Hong Kong Internment, 1942-1945: Life in the Japanese Civilian Camp at Stanley*
Patrick Boniface – *HMS Cumberland*, p9
George Wright-Nooth – *Prisoner of the Turnip Heads: Horror, Hunger and Humour in Hong Kong, 1941-1945*
Gwulo: Old Hong Kong – https://gwulo.com
Industrial History of Hong Kong – https://industrialhistoryhk.org

EXPLORE ASIA WITH BLACKSMITH BOOKS

From booksellers around the world or from *www.blacksmithbooks.com*